COUNSELING
WITH
COLLEGE
STUDENTS

SUCCESSFUL PASTORAL COUNSELING SERIES

COUNSELING WITH COLLEGE STUDENTS

CHARLES F. KEMP

Prentice-Hall, Inc., Englewood Cliffs, N.J.

Counseling with College Students
by Charles F. Kemp

© 1964 by Prentice-Hall, Inc., Englewood Cliffs, New
Jersey.

Library of Congress Catalog Card Number: 64–23561

Printed in the United States of America.
T 18320

PRENTICE-HALL INTERNATIONAL, INC., *London*
PRENTICE-HALL OF AUSTRALIA, PTY., LTD., *Sydney*
PRENTICE-HALL OF CANADA, LTD., *Toronto*
PRENTICE-HALL OF INDIA (PRIVATE) LTD., *New Delhi*
PRENTICE-HALL OF JAPAN, INC., *Tokyo*
PRENTICE-HALL DE MEXICO, S.A., *Mexico City*

Dedicated to
Dr. Paul Wassenich,
teacher, counselor and friend
of many students

ACKNOWLEDGMENTS

I would like to express my appreciation to Dr. Paul Wassenich, Professor of Religion and Director of the Honors Program at Texas Christian University, to The Reverend Ralph Stone, Minister to Students of the University Christian Church of Fort Worth and to Mr. and Mrs. Kenneth Lawrence, both of whom are doing graduate work at Texas Christian University in a ministry to students. Each of these persons has read the manuscript in its entirety and made many helpful suggestions. Also, I would like to express my appreciation to Dr. Russell Dicks, editor of the Successful Pastoral Counseling Series, for inviting me to share in this series and for his encouragement in the preparation of this volume.

INTRODUCTION

This series of books represents the most comprehensive publishing effort ever made in the field of pastoral care. These books could not have been published twenty-five years ago, or probably even ten, for the material was not then available. In the past, single books have been available covering different phases of the task. Now we are bringing the subjects together in a single series. Here we present a library of pastoral care covering the major topics and problems that most pastors will encounter in their ministry. Fortunately, not all of these problems need be faced every week or even every month. But, when they are, the minister wants help and he wants it immediately.

These books are prepared for the nonspecialized minister serving the local church, where he is the most accessible professional person in the community. It is a well-accepted fact that more people turn to clergy when in trouble than to all other professional people. Therefore, the pastor must not fail them.

Russell L. Dicks
General Editor

CONTENTS

Part III

THE PASTOR AND HIS METHODS

INTRODUCTION:
The PASTOR, The STUDENT And The CAMPUS

The subject of this book is pastoral counseling of university students. It is not a book that attempts to cover the whole range of a ministry to students. It is one part (the most important part, we feel) of a ministry to students.

Neither is it a book on pastoral counseling in general. There are many books in this field. Such men as Russell Dicks, Seward Hiltner, Wayne Oates and Carroll Wise have contributed good books on the subject of pastoral counseling. We will try to avoid duplication of subject matter contained in these volumes.

This is an attempt to understand the particular needs and problems in one area of pastoral counseling—pastoral counseling of students on our college and university campuses. This most important segment of our population has been largely neglected in the literature on pastoral counseling. Valuable discussions of such subjects as ministry to the sick, ministry to older people and marriage counseling have been published, but until now no volume has dealt with *pastoral* counseling of students.

Many books on counseling students—hundreds, in fact—have been written with the university counselor or faculty member in mind. They include only an occasional reference to the church or the pastor, and, although they sometimes speak of moral and spiritual values, their primary emphasis is on academic and vocational choice and personality adjustment. Again we hope to avoid duplication. We shall refer frequently to such studies, for the pastor has much to learn from university counselors and must frequently work with them. This is a book on the pastor and his opportunities and responsibilities in counseling students.

The Pastor

The truth of the matter is that many people are doing such counseling. Among them are pastors, ministers of education, ministers to students, directors of student foundations, university chaplains, directors of religious activities, secretaries of Student Christian Associations and professors of religion. Some counsel incidentally or occasionally, as a part of their other activities; some do it extensively—almost as specialists. In a variety of orientations, locations and symbolic roles, some have unique opportunities. We have all these groups in mind when we speak of the pastor, and we shall refer to several, pointing out some of the opportunities and responsibilities that are theirs.

The pastor of the local church. We shall mention first the group that exists in the greatest number—the pastors of local churches. Every pastor, no matter how remote his parish, is a potential student counselor. All churches, rural or urban, downtown or suburban, large or small, have in their membership young people who complete secondary school and attend college.

This wouldn't have been as true a generation ago as it is today. In 1900, only 4 percent of the college-age group attended colleges and universities. In 1956, 35 percent entered college. It is estimated that 50 percent will in 1970. In some communities 80 to 90 percent of all young people go on to college.[1] If a pastor has only one student who attends college and needs help, it is important. In the course of a ministry, however, the average pastor will deal with hundreds.

The pastor has an exceptional opportunity to prepare them for the experience, to counsel them as they face the questions of the value of a college education versus entering the business world after graduation from secondary school, the choice of a school, the selection of a major field of study and so forth. Some have conflicts with their parents about the value of going on to school at all. Many capable students doubt their ability to do advanced work. Some need financial help. Others are quite unprepared academically and emotionally for the experience.

The pastor has the distinct advantage of knowing them as persons, knowing their families' backgrounds and attitudes and, if his relationship with them has been good thus far, of continuing through this experience with them also.

If he is not in the same community as the campus, he has the obvious disadvantage of being separated from the student for long periods of time. Even here, however, counseling need not be completely shut off. A student will often write to a pastor in moments of discouragement or indecision, requesting his counsel and advice; when the student returns home during vacations, he may seek his guidance and help.

The pastor has two distinct advantages and opportunities. One is that he can prepare the students for the spiritual experience of the campus. As we shall see later in this study, many students have religious difficulties on the campus. This is not always the fault of the campus. Many students have not had religious backgrounds adequate to meet the challenges of the campus. This is the pastor's responsibility before the student ever leaves his home church.

The other advantage is that the pastor knows the student's family. On occasion, the pastor will have opportunity to work with the parents of a student who is having difficulty. The university counselor or the university pastor cannot see the parents unless they come to the campus. Even if he lives in the same town, he does not have the same relationship with the family that the pastor of the local church has. The parents are frequently part of the problem. They may come to their pastor when a problem arises. It can be the other way around. Knowing of a problem, the pastor can seek out the parents, because of his natural entree into the homes of his people. In helping them to understand the situation, he helps the student as well.

If he is to minister to his own students, the pastor needs to keep in touch with those who minister to them on the campus. At times such campus personnel will need to refer to him. We shall next discuss some of these positions and their opportunities.

The pastor of a university church. The pastor of a church in a university community has the same responsibilities toward the young people in his congregation as has the pastor of any local church. Many of them will not attend the school in their hometown, but some will.

He also has the additional responsibility and privilege of ministering to the students in the university community in which he preaches. They may come from all over the country. Many will attend his services. His church may become their "home away from home." If he preaches as though he was aware of their needs, if he has the reputation of one who is understanding of students, many will seek him for counseling. This is one of his great opportunities.

Dr. Harry Emerson Fosdick was a master in this field. His ministry at Riverside Church in New York City was carried on in the shadow of Columbia University and across the street from Union Theological Seminary, a very center of student life. Speaking to his congregation at Riverside, he said, "You have put me in this pulpit, in a university community, and asked me week by week to try to make the things of the spirit more real to you. By God's grace I will try. But how can I help thinking of the people, young people in particular. . . ."[2] It was his common practice in preaching to turn his attention specifically to the youth present. Such remarks as follow were common in his preaching. Speaking on the subject "Take What You Want and Pay for It," he emphasized the importance of one's choice of a life of self-sacrifice and service, or of a life of self-indulgence, by saying, "To some youth here I wish this might come home." Again, he turned from his general congregation and said, "I am talking to some youth here. Don't let this situation fool you! Evil may be sold on the installment plan, but believe me! The bills at last come in."[3] On a Palm Sunday, speaking on the subject "Crucified by Stupidity," he said, "I beg leave to speak for a moment especially to you young people. I plead with you—dare I say it?—not so much against wickedness as against stupidity. You have a great chance. How many older ones there are in this congregation who wish they had again the chance that you have now . . . to build a strong character, to live a high life, to undergird your soul with great faiths, to dedicate your life to noble ends. . . . That is not simply being good; that is being intelligent."[4]

So commonly in his preaching he revealed his concern for youth and turned his attention directly to them. Frequently in speaking to youth he challenged them to lives of service. "Every preacher has his dreams," he said, "and this is mine." Then he continued to express his desire that some young man or woman of real ability who was attending their services would, as a result, dedicate himself to a life of self-forgetful service.[5]

Because of such preaching many students sought personal interviews with him. In fact, probably one of his greatest contributions to youth was in individual interviews with young people. In an article he recalls an early experience. "A young man from one of the church's finest families sought my help. I recall my desperate feeling that if the Gospel of Christ did not have in it available power to save that youth, of what use was it? . . . months of conference and inward struggle ended in triumph when that young man said to me, 'If you ever find anyone who doesn't believe in God, send him to me . . . I know.'"[6]

Because of his location and outstanding position, he dealt with many unique situations. Young people of unusual talent from all over the world, who were studying in New York, came to him for guidance. He tells of one such situation. "A few months ago a Chinese student came to see me. He had come to America for a scientific education; now a doctor of medicine, he was an able and highly trained scientific man. But he was so spiritually hungry that he was being tempted in his extremity to turn to Christ to meet his need. Only how could he, with his scientific mind, become a Christian? So, drawn to it, he still rebelled against it and, like Paul, at first was scornful of Christianity even while he came to me wistfully to talk about it. A letter has just come from that man, a medical officer now with one of our units in Australia. . . . 'Ever grateful for the talk with you,' he writes, 'always remember your help. Glad to say that I have found the Something I longed for.'"[7]

The pastor in the university church has the very real advantage of being available to students. He is there; they need not depend on correspondence or wait for a trip home to see him. He also has the advantage of knowing the college atmosphere, being acquainted with university personnel and having access to information about the student and to sources of referral. While he doesn't have the local pastor's advantage (except for his own congregation) of knowing the families, he does have the advantage of anonymity. Sometimes it is easier for a student to reveal some of his doubts, problems and uncer-

tainties to a stranger than it is to the home pastor, simply because the
university pastor is not likely to see the parents and does not know
the student's background. Also, the student may not feel that he is
going against his traditional beliefs and so forth so much if he discusses them with a pastor at the campus rather than at home.

One can think of some outstanding examples of such a ministry.
Phillips Brooks had a tremendous ministry with students at Harvard.
For years he preached in the chapel and then would go to the chaplains' rooms at Wadsworth House where students would come to see
him in great numbers. They brought him all kinds of problems—
concerning morals, doubt, vocation, faith and everything else. When
he felt the time had come for this to be terminated, the students
petitioned that he should continue.

Young people from all over the country went to Boston to go to
school. Many carried letters of introduction to Phillips Brooks. His
correspondence was filled with requests from relatives and ministers
of all denominations who were concerned about various young persons. His friend and biographer, A. V. G. Allen, said, "He did not
neglect these commissions for he knew how much they meant to
those who sent them."[8] He never had a course in pastoral counseling,
but he was an extremely effective counselor because he combined a
great personal concern with common sense and a desire to understand
and a willingness to listen.

Washington Gladden had a similar influence with the students at
the State University in Columbus, Ohio. His ministry took place
during a time when questions of Biblical criticism and the relationships of science and religion were causing so much difficulty. Gladden felt an obligation to the students to face these issues squarely and
honestly. He prepared series of Sunday evening sermons to meet the
spiritual needs of students—who responded in great numbers, both in
the services and in his study.

Specialists with students: the university pastor. More recently there has been developed a specialized ministry to students,
the university pastor. Some of these workers are employed on the
staff of a large church to serve as a member of a multiple staff with
particular responsibility to students. Some are employed by denominational groups, either state or national, to serve particular groups on

the campus. Every large university is surrounded by student houses, foundations and fellowships representing all the major denominations.

This is relatively new. Clarence Shedd, in his history of a student ministry, titled *The Church Follows Its Students,* dates the movement from about 1905. Experimental work had been attempted at the University of Illinois, the University of Michigan and the University of Texas prior to 1900. In 1903 the General Assembly of the Presbyterian Church U.S.A. appointed a special committee to investigate the possibility of appointing "Special ministers who shall reside in and care for the Presbyterian students in state universities, very much after the pattern of army and navy chaplains."[9]

In 1905 The Reverend J. Leslie French was the first Presbyterian pastor to be called to serve at the University of Michigan. Since then the practice has grown by leaps and bounds. Today each denomination has its university pastors. The work of these men is quite varied and extensive, but from the beginning a large portion of it was conceived to be in the field of religious counseling and guidance. As early as 1911, Dr. Richard C. Hughes, in a report to the board of the Presbyterian Church U.S.A., said, "Nothing will take the place of personal face-to-face dealing with each student by a strong, mature man who knows the meaning and the value of life and who has wisdom and experience enough to do this difficult and delicate work."[10]

The "face-to-face" ministry to students is still one of the greatest responsibilities of the university pastor. He has some distinct advantages, chief of which is the fact that he gives full time to students. One of the problems of the pastor of a university church is that he is so busy with sermon preparation, administrative responsibilities and so forth that the time he has available for students may be limited. The university pastor, however, can give his full time to students. He is related to the campus but is not identified with such matters as the giving of grades and discipline. He has the resources of small group discussions, fellowship and worship groups that can be used to supplement his counseling.

He does have the limitation, though it need not be serious, of being identified with one particular denominational group.

Specialists with students: the university chaplain. Another
form of specialized ministry to students is the university chaplain. He
differs from the university pastor in that he does not represent a denomination or a group of denominations but the administration of
the university. This has both advantages and disadvantages. His is an
ecumenical ministry. His identification with the administration may
create some barriers. At the same time it gives him a natural relationship with the university personnel services and, on some campuses,
he is considered a member of the personnel staff and, in a few, a
member of the counseling staff.

This is a relatively new development. Yale University had a chaplain as early as 1775, but only recently have such men been employed
in any significant number. This new emphasis began about 1920
and has accelerated greatly since World War II. Seymour Smith, in
his study titled *The American College Chaplaincy*, speaks of a national conference of college chaplains and directors of religious life
that, held at Yale in 1948, drew an attendance of more than one
hundred.[11] Undoubtedly there were many who could not attend.
Smith's study, which appeared in 1954 and covered 406 colleges and
universities, most of which were independent or church-related,
found that 185 had chaplains on their staffs. This would be a little
less than 50 percent, but undoubtedly this percentage would be
higher today.

These persons are known by a variety of titles. We have used the
term *chaplain* because it is the most common. On some campuses,
where it is appropriate, he is known as "the dean of the chapel"; at
others he is called "the director of religious life," or "the director of
religious activities"; on some campuses he is referred to as "college
pastor" or "college preacher." On some campuses he teaches part time
in the department of religion or philosophy. On some campuses he
has regular preaching responsibilities; on some he does not. From the
standpoint of this study, on most campuses he is involved in personal
counseling. About one-third of the chaplains in Smith's study made
sick calls in the university infirmary. They all did personal counseling. Most of them averaged more than thirty students per month, and
some (15 percent) saw more than one hundred per month. Much of
this is of a theological or religious nature, yet chaplains are also consulted about academic, vocational and personal problems.

Specialists with students: Student Christian Association secretaries. We include Y.M.C.A., Y.W.C.A. and Student Christian Association secretaries (where the work is combined) because a large percentage of such workers are ordained and the Student Christian Associations are primarily religious groups. Actually they were the first in the field, even preceding university personnel services in many cases. Many of the programs pioneered by the student "Y," such as student unions, courses in marriage and individual counseling, were later taken over by the university and other religious groups.

Early religious influences in state universities were carried on almost exclusively by the "Y." Harvard had a student Christian group in the 1700's, with Cotton Mather as "friend and counselor," but the first official student "Y" is credited to the University of Michigan in 1858. The next year a similar group was formed at the University of Virginia; since then the idea has spread very rapidly.

Most of these men were religiously trained, ordained clergymen and were accepted by both the churches and the schools as the representatives of religion on the campus. The two best known men were, of course, John R. Mott and Robert E. Speer.

Both men were men of great intellectual ability. Both had a personal struggle about their own life work. Both men changed their plans while in college. Mott had intended to go into business; Speer to enter law. Both had a tremendous platform appeal to students and a great capacity to work with students as individuals.

This was especially true of Mott. He literally traveled the world over. Probably no man spoke to as many students on as many different campuses as John R. Mott. Effective as he was from the platform and although he had a genius for organization, he became increasingly aware of the value of individual face-to-face contacts. Basil Mathews describes one of his speaking tours, which happened to be at Edinburgh but was characteristic of those on other campuses. He quotes Mott's comments on the Edinburgh sojourn: "I then fixed interviews in a neighboring hotel with men who wished to see me. There were so many . . . that I limited men to ten or fifteen minutes each, although in certain cases I extended the time. My interviews that night kept me from 9:30 P.M. to 1:00 A.M. On Monday morning I devoted about three hours to similar interviews. . . . Three hours more in the afternoon were given to interviews. In all I had forty interviews with these inquirers."[12] Mathews feels this was, perhaps, the most significant contribution of Mott's extensive travels. "In the lives of many all across the world, however, the priceless gift of this travel has been the enheartening cheer and renewal of courage that his personal affectionate counsel and comradeship have given."[13]

While there have been few men of the dynamic influence and personal charm of Mott and Speer in the "Y" or any other place, the Student Christian Associations have been a source of much helpful counsel and guidance. Their very ambiguity has helped with some students. They are on the campus but not of the administration. They are related to the church but not limited by denominational or creedal positions. They have been in a unique position to be of assistance to foreign students, many of whom knew of the "Y" in their own countries.

Professors of religion.   The primary responsibility of the professor of religion is teaching. However, he also may do much counseling, and because of the fact that he is usually ordained and a teacher in the area of religion, it may be primarily pastoral counseling. (All professors do counseling. We deal with that in a later section. We are including professors of religion here because, in many respects, their role is pastoral.)

There was a time in the history of higher education when counseling responsibilities were assumed by a large percentage of the faculty. Edmund G. Williamson, writing of the history of student personnel work, refers to the early American university when "faculties were composed largely of soul-centered clergymen, enrollments were small, and professors were more interested in teaching individual students than in prosecuting research. . . . The development of the *whole* student—mind, body and soul—was the chief objective, and instructional techniques were, for the most part, individualized."[14]

One should not minimize the contribution of such men. Washington Gladden tells of the influence in his life of one teacher who did much to challenge him to greater efforts. There was a time when he was seemingly making little progress in school. Speaking of the difficulty he found in applying himself to study, he said, "But the teacher to whom I have referred, after some discouraging failures, succeeded in kindling my ambition. My debt to him is greater than I could ever hope to repay. . . . His power of arousing and inspiring students, of appealing to all that was best in them, of making fine ideals of conduct attractive to them was quite exceptional. He found me a listless and lazy pupil; he left me with a zest for study and a firm purpose of self-improvement. It was a clear case of conversion, and when anyone tells me that character cannot be changed through the operation of spiritual forces, I know better."[15]

Dr. Fosdick said the most important single influence of his college career, especially when he was having difficulties with his religious thinking, was simply the presence of William Newton Clarke on the campus.[16] He knew that the latter had wrestled with all the issues of doubt and faith and the very fact that he was there was important.

Those who are carrying on a teaching ministry have some unique advantages. The fact that they are on the faculty gives them authority in the eyes of some. They can surround their counseling, especially on religious problems, with their courses. They have the time and opportunity to work through some of these problems rather extensively and thoroughly. Through class discussion, reading and writing assignments they can help the student face issues thoroughly in a way that the pastor can never do in one or two interviews. It is true that students' feelings need to worked through and their doubts need to be expressed, but this can be done in the interview. Furthermore, it is done in the context of a class, and the student is aware that others face the same confusion and uncertainty. This can do much to relieve the sense of loneliness and guilt.

Visiting preachers and pastors. There are occasions when pastors from any one of the previously mentioned categories are called upon to visit a campus as a guest lecturer, preacher in chapel or as a member of a team for a religion-in-life week emphasis. Most campuses carry on such a program.

This, too, can lead to counseling. Washington Gladden not only worked with the students at Columbus but was a frequent preacher and lecturer on campuses throughout America. He served for a time as visiting preacher at Harvard and there, like Brooks, met students in Wadsworth House who wanted to discuss their personal problems with him. This, he felt, was the most significant part of his responsibility. They brought him a variety of problems—academic, vocational and personal. On one occasion, he said, "I began to understand the value of the confessional."[17]

One of the most effective of such visitors was Henry Drummond. Drummond was not a pastor of a church but was something of a combination of evangelist, scientist, teacher, author, lecturer, counselor and friend of youth on three continents. He had almost phenomenal success in talking to students.

George Adam Smith, his biographer and friend, said that to associate him with mass meetings, where he was so effective, was to misrepresent him. His greatest contribution, Smith said, was the great number of personal interviews he granted to students who sought them. In Smith's words, "One who heard Drummond through several years of the Student Movement said there was one power that distinguished him beyond every other preacher to men, and that was the power of so speaking as invariably to move from one hundred to two hundred of his audience of seven or eight hundred not merely to stay to an after-meeting but to talk to him one by one and face to face. This power never failed him with the students and it was by it he left an abiding mark on hundreds of lives."[18]

Wherever he went students sought to talk with him. He tells in a letter of scheduling interviews with students until late at night and hardly finding time to carry on his correspondence. He was constantly seen walking with some student on the campus or engaged in conversation in some dormitory at all hours of the day or night.

Such counseling is necessarily short-term and has great limitations, yet it does point up a need and at times is effective. When John R. Mott was a student at Cornell University J. K. Studd, the former athlete from England, spoke on the campus. Mott was then experiencing his own struggle about what he should do and be. He even hesitated about attending the service but decided to go, even though he went late. That night the speaker challenged him as he had never been challenged before. Studd made three statements which, Mott said, proved to be the turning point in his life. They were: "Seekest thou great things for thyself? Seek them not. Seek first the 'kingdom of God.'" He said he forgot all else the speaker said but "on these few words hinged my life investment decision."[19] He went back to his room to ponder the problem. The next day he sought out the speaker for an interview. There was an entry in Studd's diary, "At 2:30 I had a visit from Mott, talked on Christian work." There is no way Studd could have realized the far-reaching consequences of that interview.

There is no way any pastor can tell the far-reaching consequences of any interview with any student.

The Student

More than four million students are on our college and university campuses. Both the total number and the percentage in comparison with the general population continue to increase each year. This is one of the largest subgroups in our society, a subgroup which Dr. Kate Herner Mueller of Indiana University says "differentiated sharply from any other community of a similar size."[20]

Yet, while it is true that students constitute a subgroup, it is deceiving to think of them as having common characteristics and patterns. Perhaps no group is as diversified as are students on a college campus. Some are freshmen, new and confused; some are seniors or graduate students, sophisticated and wise to the ways of the campus. Some are on academic probation; some are Phi Beta Kappa candidates, regularly on the Dean's List. Some are homesick; others are glad to escape the restraints of home. Some are wrapped up in fraternity and sorority life; some are totally uninterested and look upon Greek letter societies with disdain. Some are primarily interested in athletics; others, in drama and the other fine arts. Some have clear-cut vocational goals and ambitions; others have no vocational plans at all. Some find it necessary to work to scrape together enough to pay tuition and buy books; others come from wealthy homes and drive their own convertibles to the campus. Some are married; others are single. Some are well adjusted and mature; others are quite disturbed and subject to constant anxiety and strain. Some are very popular, living in a social whirl; others prefer to be alone. Still others spend weekends in the dorm—not by choice but because no one asks them out. Some find college challenging; others find it boring. Some will graduate with honors; many will flunk out. Who can say what a student is or what he is like?

The one element common to all students is the fact that all are engaged in academic pursuits. This doesn't mean that all of them are there for the love of learning. Far from it! Some are there because it's "the thing to do," or because one is likely to get a better job, or because their parents wanted them to attend. Some are there primarily to play football; others, for the social life—or, as one girl said, "Frankly, I didn't come to college to get an education, but a husband." Nevertheless, they all must register for classes. Fortunately, some see the purpose and value of an education and are there to learn.

Generally speaking, one can say that students represent an age group. Not all young people of college age are in college, but, by and large, the student group represents a relatively brief span of years, roughly from seventeen to the early twenties. However, this is changing. With the increasing emphasis on graduate programs, more older people are appearing on the campus and in the college classroom. Mueller presents the surprising statistic that the age range of 17 through 22 constitutes only 63 percent of the college population.[21]

It can also be said that, as a general rule, students represent the postadolescent and young adult years. This means that the worker with students deals with no children, few teen-agers, occasional middle-aged people and practically no elder statesmen.

Students represent the upper levels of the population intellectually. They may not act like it during some escapades, such as panty raids, but they are, nonetheless. This does not mean that students represent all the upper levels. Unfortunately, far too many of college ability do not go to college. It does mean that those who are there, especially those who have survived the first year, are of the upper levels. As Florence Goodenough points out, "By the time of college entrance the steady process of screening that has been going on since the primary grades has gradually weeded out most of the subjects whose general intelligence level is much below the top quartile of the population at large. The great bulk of the college population is made up of the upper 10 percent of the general population."[22]

This means that on the campus today are the leaders of the future.

Again we must point out that all of the leaders are not on the campus. Some who are denied the advantages of a college education will rise to positions of leadership. Nevertheless, anyone working with students must be aware of the fact that he is dealing with people of great potential. The professional men, the statesmen, the leaders in church and society tomorrow are primarily on the campuses of today.

The students on our campuses come mainly from the higher economic and social levels. This is unfortunate, but true. Because of the expense involved in obtaining a college education, the majority of students come from the middle and upper classes, usually from homes of professional and semiprofessional vocations. There are notable exceptions, and there need to be more, but at the present time this is true.

It is only natural that students have problems. The very fact that they are going to school can be a problem. All periods of transition are marked by uncertainty and insecurity. Many students are away from home for the first time. Although roughly 60 percent of college students live with their parents, 40 percent live on campus.[23] Some homesickness, some breaking of moral and religious restraints is to be expected.

The fact that these students are in a certain age group gives rise to some problems. Studies in the psychology of adolescence make much of the concept of developmental tasks. Later adolescence (or the common college age) has many far-reaching developmental tasks—breaking away from family ties, gaining emotional independence, discovering new masculine and feminine roles, the choice of a life partner, the selecting of and preparing for a career, the developing of a life philosophy. Such tasks and such decisions affect a student's entire future. Some young people make these choices and adjustments quite easily; for others they are a great source of tension and, at times, pain.

In the period of later adolescence there are degrees of immaturity. It could not be otherwise. One can't have thirty years of experience by the time he is eighteen. As a result students are often hypercritical and immature in their judgments and lacking in discipline. They have abundant energy but limited experience.

The fact that the students as a whole are in the top levels intellectually creates problems for some. Many students cannot maintain the pace. Others, who may have done quite well in high school, find now a competition they have never before experienced. A high school valedictorian may find himself in a class with many valedictorians and, for the first time, may realize what it means to have others surpass him.

Some problems are seasonal. Orientation week, the first weeks of school, for the new students can be a time of great confusion and bewilderment. Social life is not all pleasant. As one person said, "Rush week is tragedy in the lives of many hundreds of persons." He referred to one campus where five hundred girls were invited to participate in rush activities, but only two hundred could be accepted by sororities. "The result was that on Tuesday too many girls cried themselves to sleep and too many parents thought of them with aching hearts."[24]

Later in the year come homesickness, the pressure for time and finals—all of which bring their own pressures and tensions.

The student experiences the necessity of reorienting his thinking intellectually, morally and spiritually. No wonder there are tensions. They differ in degree and intensity, but all students experience them at some time or other.

In terms of counseling all this means that on most campuses there are three general groups which overlap each other:

(1) There is a small group of students who will need extensive counseling. Some will need psychotherapy.

(2) There is a large group that would benefit from some counseling. They might well survive without it (indeed many of them do), but their decisions could be a bit clearer, they could live much happier lives, they could be freer from tension and guilt and, with some guidance at the right time, could be more effective students and persons.

(3) There are many students who have problems, too (as we have indicated above), but are quite capable of making their own decisions and solving their own problems.

How to help such students is the subject of the rest of this volume. First, we would do well to take a short look at the campus.

The Campus

The pastor who would work with college students must know not only the students; he must also know the campus. This is true in all special areas or institutions. The chaplain of a hospital must know the regulations, the personnel, the program of the hospital. The chaplain of a reformatory must be familiar with the atmosphere, the requirements, the nature of the institution in which he works. The military chaplain must know the military regulations, the problems of men in service and the particular and unique needs of the men in his branch of the service. Every counselor counsels within the framework of the institution of which he is a part. This is as true of a college campus as of any of the other areas mentioned. As David Boroff says, "College guidance is an art—an almost impossible art—based on incredibly complex imponderables. But it can make sense only when one knows what colleges are *really* like."[25]

He who would serve on a campus must know something of higher education—its nature, its goals, its history, its purposes. He not only should know something of higher education in general, he must know his own campus in particular. While all campuses have some things in common, they also are quite different. They vary in size, in geographical location, in admission policies, in sponsorship and affiliation, in tuition rates, in curriculum offerings, in tradition—all these things make a difference in the life of the student.

After all, there are more than two thousand colleges in America. We would not expect them all to be alike. Colleges, like churches, have personalities all their own. Some are friendly, others are impersonal; some are highly intellectual, others may have much lower standards. Some lay great stress on athletics; others may have no athletic program at all. All this is to be expected when we consider that higher education in America throughout its history has tried to meet the needs of a vast number of religious, cultural and economic groups.

What are some of these differences?

Size is the most obvious. Schools vary from small denominational schools, with enrollments of two or three hundred, to huge state uni-

versities with student bodies of twenty or thirty thousand. The trend
is probably toward the large campus. Although only 8½ percent of
the colleges enroll more than five thousand students, these include
more than 53 percent of all students. Only 6 percent of the students
in America are in schools under five hundred in enrollment, yet this
includes 45 percent of all institutions. The approximately 40 percent
remaining are enrolled in schools with enrollments from five hundred
to five thousand.

The size of the school influences the size of the classes, the chance
to participate in activities, the individual attention one receives from
professors, the opportunity to know professors at all. Mueller feels
that "perhaps the major difference between the large and the small
college lies essentially in the greater amount of self-reliance and ag-
gressiveness required on the large campus. Every student needs at
least one wise and warm-hearted friend, either teacher or student, if
his heart as well as his head is to be in his work . . . in the large and
unselected student group that friend may be harder to find and easier
to lose."[26]

In terms of counseling, the large university may have more facilities, more full-time personnel staff available. The small school may
have more informal contacts between professor and student, more
opportunities for friendly guidance, but fewer specially trained counseling personnel. There are obvious exceptions to both cases.

The geographical location also influences the cultural patterns.
Whether the campus is in the North, South, East, or West, Midwest
or Southwest makes a difference. Whether it is in a small rural town,
in the heart of a city as are Columbia and Pittsburgh, for example, or
in a suburban area also influences the pattern of life. A municipal
university may have a completely transient student body whose members spend much time commuting. There is usually very little sense
of student-body solidarity. Boroff contrasts such schools as Harvard,
Wisconsin, Claremont and Swarthmore, which draw students with a
wide variety of environmental and cultural backgrounds from all over
the nation, with such schools as Brooklyn College in New York, Parsons College in rural Iowa or Birmingham-Southern, all of which
attract students primarily from their local environment.[27]

Differences in admission policies have a great influence on the groups that comprise the student body. Some schools, like Oberlin and Rice, are highly selective. Others, particularly state schools, admit almost any high school graduate, going by the philosophy that "anyone has a right to flunk out." It is not our purpose to argue which is preferable. Much can be said on both sides. Each has values; each has limitations. However, these admission policies do influence the type of students and the general atmosphere of the campus. Mueller points out that the highly selective school that admits no one below the top quartile of high school graduates develops a rather parochial outlook. This is especially true if a high admissions standard is coupled with a high tuition rate. These schools have automatically eliminated three-fourths of the population, to begin with: those below the top quartile, and only that portion of the remainder that have the finances required.

Some schools admit only men, others only women, although the vast majority of campuses are coeducational.

The curriculum also determines, to a large extent, the nature of the student body and the atmosphere of the campus. An agricultural college is quite different from a school of engineering. On large university campuses all kinds of programs are offered and all kinds of degrees are available, both graduate and undergraduate. The catalogs of some of our larger universities, such as Columbia, Minnesota, Michigan and Stanford, look like mail order catalogs and include almost as many items. Many schools specialize in one area; for example, teachers' colleges or agricultural colleges. To make the picture complete we must include professional schools, such as schools of medicine, dentistry, law, nursing and theology.

There are also numerous graduate schools, such as those at Johns Hopkins, Harvard, Yale and most state universities. These offer a variety of graduate degrees in a rapidly growing number of fields of specialization.

In addition, the growing number of junior, or two-year colleges, includes those that offer a general liberal arts program and numerous trade schools. The junior college arose to meet a need. It was felt that for many young people the standard four-year college covered too long a period; also, some students were graduating from high school too young. For many, the junior college leads to a culminating degree. For others, it leads to a four-year college. This latest member of the American higher education scene has grown very rapidly. In fact, one out of every four college students is attending a junior college.

Here they are, vastly different: large and small; in North and South, East and West; male, female and coeducational; four-year; graduate and undergraduate; high standards and low; expensive and inexpensive; liberal arts and professional; friendly and impersonal; rural, urban and suburban; church-related and state-sponsored—each with its own culture, environment and mores. We should avoid stereotypes. Not all large campuses are cold and impersonal. Not all small campuses are warm and friendly. Not all church-related campuses have a vital religious influence. Not all state schools are without religious values. Each campus must be seen in its own right and understood by those who work there.

One thing is certain—most students at times need a friend and counselor.

Ordway Tead says one of the great needs on our campuses is for someone to care about each student, and how he is developing. This, he says, is a "must." But he acknowledges, "How we can achieve that in huge student bodies it is not easy to see, unless a wholly new emphasis in relations with students is aggressively developed. . . ." Yet he continues, "There is no escape from the psychic reality that if there is to be guided growth, some individual, warm of heart and wise of mind, should be the guide, counselor and friend of every student."[28]

Perhaps the pastor can be that friend.

COUNSELING
WITH
COLLEGE
STUDENTS

Part I

UNDERSTANDING THE STUDENT

CHAPTER ONE

THE AVERAGE STUDENT:
HIS NEEDS And PROBLEMS

It is difficult to separate needs and problems. When a need is not met, it becomes a problem. Students, like all other segments of the population, have both. There have been various attempts to classify student problems. E. G. Williamson, in one of the early books on student counseling, divided student problems into four major areas: personality problems, problems of educational orientation and achievement, problems of occupational orientation, financial and health problems.[1] Gilbert Wrenn, in his book *Student Personnel Work in College*, lists the following as specific needs, often referred to as problems: academic problems, vocational problems, financial problems, social problems and emotional problems.[2] Each of these divisions has several subheadings.

Various checklists of problems have been developed and administered to students. The University of Minnesota has one that includes thirty-three items. The familiar Mooney problem checklist has frequently been used. Such surveys reveal that students do not have *a* problem, but problems. A study conducted by Francis R. Robinson of Ohio State University, showed that students will mark an average of twenty-five problems each.[3] These are distributed in such areas as adjustment to college life, personal psychological relations, vocational and educational failure, social and recreational activities, health and physical development, curriculum and teaching procedures, social-psychological relations, courtship, sex, marriage, finances, living conditions and employment, home and family, morals and religion. This in itself is quite a list.

Other surveys produce similar results. They are suggestive as to the degree and wide range of problems that exist on our campuses. They range all the way from relatively minor matters, such as the choice of a course or learning to take notes effectively in class, to major problems of life adjustment and commitment that may affect a student's entire future.

It should be pointed out also that many students are not aware of the true nature of their problems. A study conducted on five different campuses pointed out that a large percentage of students who had received counseling had a different conception of what their problem was from what the counselor later found it to be.[4]

Much depends on the person's point of view. If one would ask administrators what the major problems of students are, many would say they are financial and disciplinary. Professors might feel they are problems of maturation and study habits. Counselors and psychiatrists would undoubtedly emphasize that the problems are rooted in conflicting emotions and personal maladjustment. Pastors might feel that basically it is a matter of spiritual misunderstanding and a lack of clarity about the meaning of life.

We recognize that all classifications are artificial and, in actual experience, overlap. A family problem may have great influence on academic achievement. Unrealistic educational or vocational goals may result in real emotional difficulties. It is only for purposes of discussion that they can be separated. There are at least five general areas in which a pastor on a campus is likely to be faced with problems of his students. These areas are academic, vocational, premarital and marital, personal or emotional and spiritual.

Academic Problems

It is only to be expected that many students will have academic problems. One study conducted jointly at Ohio State University and the University of Colorado indicated that these are more prevalent than any other problem.[5] This is evident in the number of dropouts.

A news release from the Southern Regional Education Board began, "Behind every student who paraded in cap and gown at Commencement recently walked the shadow of another who entered college at the same time but dropped out." Of all freshmen entering in a given year, 27 percent drop out before the year is over, 42 percent have dropped out by the end of the second year, 48 percent by the

end of the third year and 55 percent by the end of the fourth year.[6]
This may be due to a lack of ability, a lack of funds, a lack of motivation. There are many reasons why students drop out of school. Some
were poor college risks to begin with; some never learned to study;
some never found a program which really interested them; some were
disturbed by personal and family problems; some attempted too many
other activities; some had a work load that was too heavy. Each person had his own reasons. Each experienced disappointment, frustration and discouragement. Each dropout meant a certain amount of
time and effort wasted, a change in plans, a readjustment.

One cannot help raising certain questions. Would counseling have
helped? How many could have been saved to continue their plans
and to realize their goals if someone could have helped? How many
had any help at all? Who will do the counseling now? Who will help
them as they leave the campus to reformulate their plans, to face
their discouragement, to find new goals and objectives? How many
could be salvaged and could return to school? What is the pastor's
place in all of this?

The pastor is not an educational counselor in the technical sense of
the word. Educational counseling is in itself a specialty requiring
considerable training, skill and experience. It requires a knowledge of
psychological tests and their interpretation. It requires a thorough
knowledge of the curriculum both as to specific courses and to special
areas or plans of study. It demands a familiarity with prerequisites,
the sequence of courses, what courses lead to further training and to
vocational competence and opportunities. The educational counselor
must deal with such subtle and complex problems as the discrepancy
between educational ambitions and achievements, inappropriate educational goals, the ever-present and always puzzling problems of over-
achievement and underachievement. His task requires a thorough
knowledge of educational techniques, study habits, the scheduling of
time, conducting research, the preparation of manuscripts and the
use of the library. The academic counselor must know school traditions, customs and regulations, the meaning of academic probation;
he must be aware of the practices of other schools, for students frequently transfer from one school to another.

The causes of academic difficulty are multitudinous. The good academic counselor must be able to diagnose and determine whether academic difficulty is due to limitations of ability, a lack of motivation, inappropriate educational goals, ignorance of study procedures, personal or emotional involvements, reading disabilities or any one of a number of other causes or combination of causes that might be present.

Then the counselor must work through with the student an educational program that meets his needs, is in line with his interests and is directed toward his goals and purposes. He must help the student move toward it with an optimum of satisfaction and efficiency.

The pastor has definite and obvious limitations in such areas. Misinformation, or incomplete information, in some of these areas is worse than none at all. The pastor does not need to be an academic counselor. He does need to know his own limitations, and he needs to know that there are academic counselors. Probably the number of students who receive the level of academic counseling that we have described here is small; nevertheless, this counseling is usually available to some degree and the results of good educational guidance can be quite remarkable.

Dr. Ruth Strang tells of a college freshman girl who had such poor grades in her first two semesters that, according to the rules of the school, she should have been dropped. However, since her high school record had been good and her scholastic aptitude tests indicated she could do the work, and since she expressed a desire to try, it was decided she would be allowed to continue. Special guidance resources were made available, although she herself could determine what she would use.

In high school her work had been so easy that she could get good grades without too much effort. Consequently, her study methods were never developed. A reading test indicated she was low in reading comprehension. She was helped in improving her reading and in scheduling her time, in taking notes that would make her studying more effective. As a result, her achievement in her academic work improved, and with this improvement came a renewed interest in her work and in her college experience. She even found that it was fun to study. With a better record came a renewed confidence. She lost some of her shyness and began to take a more active part in her classes. In short, a girl who might otherwise have been dropped was enabled to continue her education and benefit from it because she received the individual help that she needed.[7]

This girl is typical of many students who either never had to, or at least never did, learn how to study in high school. The more gifted students may have found work in high school so easy that they never found it necessary to do a great deal of work. In fact, Dr. Mueller states, ". . . only a few teen-agers, relatively speaking, have been asked to make an all-out effort," and Ruth Strang estimates that from one-third to one-half of high school students do not do work commensurate with their ability.[8] It is no wonder that when they get to college they find they have academic problems.

The important thing is that these students can be helped. One of the pastor's contributions can be to see that they get the guidance they need. Strange as it may seem, they may not know that this help is available. This is particularly true of freshmen. Often they are reluctant to seek help or to accept it. Since many are unfamiliar with guidance in high school, they may not feel it will have any value. If the pastor can be the means of letting them express some of their frustrations, discouragements and hostilities and can encourage them to accept guidance—making it seem worthwhile—he can be a benefit both to the student and to the school.

The pastor may have another and a more important service to render on academic matters. No problem is exclusively academic. Many scholastic difficulties are due to emotional involvements. A student may have a high scholastic aptitude; he may have a good knowledge of study skills and techniques, but if he does not have the motivation to try, or if he is troubled by personal problems or feelings of doubt and guilt, so that he cannot keep his mind on his work, he will still have trouble in school in spite of his abilities. Academic success depends as much upon a sense of purpose, the ability to continue in spite of discouragement and upon a feeling that it is worthwhile as it does on study skills. A reasonable freedom from worry and tension may be as important a factor in a student's academic progress as the use of the library or scheduling time for study. If a student has such feelings of inadequacy that he is afraid to recite in class, or if he is so involved in a family conflict that he cannot concentrate, he will not profit much from any study methods.

Underachievement, which causes educators so much concern, may be caused by many factors. In each case they are complicated, complex and interrelated. With some it may be lack of ability; with some an inadequate background in such basic areas as English or math; with some, limitations in reading speed and comprehension. Some problems may be due to lack of confidence; some to lack of interest. Some students have problems because they do not like school; some may be homesick; others may be unpopular and thus not enjoy school; some may have been forced to go to a school they did not want to attend. Some may be carrying too much outside work. Others may be too involved in athletics or other activities on campus. The list is endless. It illustrates how complicated the problem can be and the necessity for counseling. Each case is unique and must be seen in its own light.

Since motivation and personal adjustment are such important factors, the pastor has a significant role. He specializes in such things as self-acceptance, interpersonal relationships, life's meaning, purposes and goals. Here the pastor, the professor and the school counselor can pool their resources. They should not compete with each other or duplicate each other's work. Each from his own perspective complements and reinforces the others.

Despite the best of efforts, some students fail. The tragic thing is that many failures could have been avoided, if someone had been interested enough and skilled enough to help. Even among Terman's famous gifted children, some failed in college. Each failure is a loss to society and has its own story of frustration, embarrassment, disappointment and difficulty. Some cannot help but fail. They have undertaken tasks that require more ability than they possess. Not everyone is capable of doing college-level work, but in our society there exists a rather common belief—that everyone ought to try. These people, too, have their problems—emotional, vocational, family and personal.

How do they explain their failure to their families and friends? What do they do now? Many feel they are "failures." They feel the label is permanent. Who counsels them? Who helps them reshape their plans? Regain some incentive? Restore their self-confidence and sense of worth?

In every failure, whether it is in a course, an examination or in a total program, the first step is to determine the cause or causes. As with underachievement and dropouts, the causes are multiple. The counselor or pastor needs to know whether it was due to lack of ability or effort, whether the problem is one of lack of skill or confidence. All the things mentioned earlier regarding underachievement apply to failure.

Failure is more acute and more disrupting. It is more likely to result in family conflict and difficulty. It affects the student's self-concept, his sense of confidence, his sense of worth. This may necessitate his changing both his educational and vocational goals.

This person needs counseling, especially if he needs to be rerouted. There are some whose careers can be salvaged, who can return to school, even if it is necessary to wait out a suspension period, and resume their plans. Some may need to find another major, another department or another school more in line with their interests and abilities. Some have even learned, as a result of such an experience, to become far more effective.

It is well to remember that Thomas Edison, Louis Pasteur, Fritz Kreisler, Albert Schweitzer and many others had difficulty in school. If we can provide the necessary guidance and encouragement, many students will continue, in spite of problems, underachievement and even failure, to make contributions far beyond anything we might have dreamed.

The pastor does not function as an academic counselor unless he is also on the faculty. Others are trained to do this. He should know them and work with them. He must work within the framework of the institution to which he ministers. If a student is on academic probation, the pastor may feel the regulations are too strict or too lenient, but he must understand them and accept their reality. He may want to discuss, or even suggest, changes in policy, but this is done with the administration, not with the student. The pastor recognizes that he serves as a pastor, but this need not separate him from the academic program. Working within his own area of competence and in terms of his informal relationship with students, he may make a very valuable contribution to their lives that results not only in academic achievement but in achievement in life as well.

Vocational Problems

Centuries ago Cicero said, "We must decide what manner of men we wish to be and what calling in life we would follow, and this is the most difficult problem in the world." The students on our campuses are at the age and the place in life when they are making this decision. Whether or not they feel it is the most difficult in the world would be subject to debate, but research and clinical reports would agree that many find it one of the most difficult problems they face.

It is also one of the most important decisions a student makes. His entire future will be influenced by his decision. He will live a different kind of life, depending upon whether he decides to be an engineer, a doctor, a statesman or a coach. His happiness and satisfaction in life will be largely determined by whether or not he chooses a vocation that is in line with his interests, his capabilities, his abilities, his philosophy of life, his goals and his ideals. His contribution to society, his sense of meaning and purpose will also be affected by his sense of calling or his sense of vocation. This is one of the reasons that student counseling is so important. Students are at the age when this decision is being made, and the results are so far-reaching and so very important.

We are thinking here in terms of counseling of college students by a pastor or a religious worker. This puts definite limits on our discussion. It limits the scope of vocations under consideration. The high school counselor must include the whole range of occupational choice. Students are primarily thinking in terms of the professions, highly skilled trades and management positions. They are considering occupations that require high levels of skill and extensive training.

The fact that we are thinking in terms of a pastor also limits our discussion. He is not a professional vocational counselor, but a pastor. What is his relationship to the field of vocational guidance? Should he enter into it at all? Should he send all persons with a vocational problem to a vocational counselor?

Some pastors are situated in places where vocational counselors are not available. As rapidly as personnel work has grown, there are still not enough vocational counselors to go around. The pastor may of necessity have to deal with this problem. A more common situation arises because vocational problems are so very seldom presented in isolation. They are part of a family problem, an ethical problem or even a theological one.

A student who is having difficulty with his father discusses it with his pastor. One of the problems, among others, is that his father wants him to study law, but he wants to study music. You can't separate the two. To deal with the family problem the counselor has to deal with the question of vocational choice, and vice versa.

Another student, who is engaged to a girl on the campus, wants to be a missionary; she doesn't. He has a sense of calling and commitment; he is also in love with the girl. There are many times when the pastor, because of his relationship with students, and because he is discussing other problems with them, finds that he must also become involved in the field of vocational choice. Furthermore, from our point of view, vocational choice is basically a religious matter. The very term "vocation" is a theological term. For this reason the pastor has an emphasis and a perspective that other counselors often do not have.

He may wish to refer these students to a vocational counselor for a battery of tests or for vocational counseling, for that matter, but he still has a relationship to maintain. This is another advantage of working on a campus. The pastor on a campus has sources of referral; the pastor in a local church does not have.

In one field of vocational guidance the pastor is considered the expert; that is the field of church vocations. The university counselors are not aware of the denominational differences in the concept of the ministry, the requirements for ordination or of the many seminaries in which such training can be secured. They often do not understand what is meant by a "call" to the ministry and are not familiar with the variety of opportunities the ministry offers, in addition to preaching and religious education.

If the pastor is going to accept responsibility in this very important area, he should understand the nature of vocational choice, the principles of vocational guidance and the method of working cooperatively with the rest of the campus so that he doesn't do more harm than good.

Vocational choice demands a thorough understanding of one's self. It means that one must understand his own strengths and weaknesses, his potentialities and his limitations, his likes and dislikes, his hopes and dreams, his ambitions and his goals. He must also understand the whole world of work. Out of a multitude of possible alternatives, he must select one occupation or family of occupations in which he will secure training and to which he will commit himself. This means that he should have a thorough knowledge of what this decision involves. If he chooses a particular field, he should know how he will spend his time, with whom he will be associated, what its satisfactions and dissatisfactions are (both are important). He should know what training is demanded, what the future of the field is and whether or not it renders a service to society.

Students often do not know either. They choose vocations that require more ability than they have or are not in line with their real interests. Studies show that even in the senior year of college many students are quite uninformed as to the real nature of the work they will do in the field they are studying.

The task of the vocational counselor, then, can briefly be stated in two phrases: (1) To help the student, by any means available, to understand himself realistically and maturely. (2) To help him explore and understand the vocational opportunities so that he can make a realistic decision that is mature and relatively permanent.

The vocational counselor has definite means and techniques for understanding the student. He can administer a battery of tests that will provide standardized information about abilities, vocational interests and aptitudes. He has transcripts and grade averages to evaluate. He has recent, accurate, up-to-date files of "occupational information" that can help the student understand the implications of a vocational decision.

Because of the importance of such information about both the student and the world of work, some vocational counselors feel that the pastor should not attempt this kind of counseling at all. They have a real point. To attempt to counsel a person without knowledge of his abilities, interests and so forth is not only poor counseling but is professionally irresponsible. Not to provide occupational information when it is available or worse, to provide information that is inaccurate or out-of-date, is to do more harm than good.

The pastor must be aware that such services and such information is available. He should not attempt to be a vocational counselor when he is not. For the reasons stated above, he cannot separate himself from vocational problems. We grant that the vocational counselor has techniques the pastor does not have, but the pastor may have a relationship that the vocational counselor does not have. Both are important.

The answer would seem to be in a close cooperation between the two, each performing the function he can do best. At times the pastor may refer completely to the counseling service. In other instances, as in the case of the young man considering missions, the pastor may refer to a battery of tests that evaluate the student; he then proceeds with the counseling.

We will not attempt to discuss the infinite variety of complicated vocational problems that exist on almost any campus. Some students need no vocational guidance. Their decisions are clear in their own minds; they have selected appropriate courses of preparation and are moving toward their goals. Others have what appear to be cases of vocational indecision. They simply cannot make up their minds. They may change their majors two or even three times as their interests shift. This may be due to the fact that they simply cannot settle on one of a rather wide variety of possibilities—and thus great uncertainty results. It may be related to a more profound and far-reaching problem of attempting to find a goal and purpose in life. As mentioned earlier, some students have vocational problems that are complicated by difficult interpersonal relations. These include conflict with parents, differences with a fiancée and so on. The father who wants his son to come into the firm—but the son wants to go into social work; the student whose fiancée wants him to be a doctor—but he wants to teach. All such problems complicate and confuse vocational choice.

There are many who have made, or are proposing to make, unrealistic vocational choices. Many have been misguided into a field to gratify their parents or some overly zealous recruiter. The student is unhappy in his program of preparation and doesn't exactly know why. Some who have chosen fields because of the glamour or prestige associated with them find their basic interests are not in accord with the demands of these jobs. Many girls who choose nursing as a career are really attracted by the uniform—or the interns. Some have unrealistic goals, like the student who wants to secure a Ph.D. in philosophy in order to teach, when grades and other factors indicate that he is not Ph.D. material. Some already find themselves in fields for which they are not qualified. The prelaw student who cannot keep pace with his class and the premedical student who can't pass chemistry face the necessity of rethinking their careers, their educational plans, their life goals and ambitions.

Some students, whose vocational problems are symptoms of emotional problems, may need psychotherapy rather than vocational guidance.

Any of these problems may come to the attention of the pastor. The biggest danger, at least one of the biggest, is oversimplification. This is an extremely complicated problem. The student himself is complex—with all of his background, ability, dreams, hopes and fears involved. The occupational world is complex; with advances in technology and increasing specialization, it becomes more complex every day. Added to this is the thought expressed previously—that this is basically a religious or spiritual matter. If God is concerned about a student's life, he is concerned as to how this student invests his future.

There is no simple solution to such a complex problem. Vocational counseling, therefore, takes time. It will not be completed in one interview or two. It means working with the student as he first tentatively explores a possibility and attempts to understand himself, and continuing with him until he finds a solution that can be a commitment. A sound realistic choice of a life calling extends over a period of time. It means that here, as in all counseling, the pastor makes use of all the resources available.

The pastor must recognize that the final decision is always the student's. He cannot, and should not, make the decision for the student. Vocational counseling is not giving one vocational advice. It is helping a person reach his own decision. Vocation means "calling." Each person must discover his own calling. This calling may be in any worthwhile field. Vocational counseling must include a Christian philosophy of all vocations. There is no such thing as sacred and secular. Sir William Osler was called to medicine as much as Phillips

Brooks was called to preach. All students need a deeper understanding of the real meaning of the word *vocation* in the religious or Christian sense.

Premarital and Marital Counseling

All of the problems of courtship and marriage are present and often accentuated on a college campus. The age of the average college student is the age when romantic interests are at their height. One of the basic developmental tasks of later adolescence, which includes most college students, is to achieve satisfactory relations with the opposite sex. The capacity to love and be loved, to understand and accept one's masculine or feminine role in life, to establish a lasting partnership with a husband or wife, based on mutual acceptance, understanding and love, is one of life's greatest values.

Dating on the campus may be as important as classwork and, in some cases, more so. It provides an escape from loneliness and a sense of personal worth; it leads to a satisfactory marriage adjustment. Dating provides many pleasures, but it also provides much anxiety and real heartache. Breaking up for some may amount to nothing more than a casual incident; for others it may take the form of a real bereavement experience.

The problems of interpersonal relations, masculine and feminine roles and understanding the place of sex in life predominate on any campus. Students, with all of their seeming self-confidence and sophistication, often are quite confused about such matters, and their lives are a mixture of curiosity, anxiety, misinformation and anticipation.

Everyone recognizes the importance of the home. Every magazine has an article on it. Judges, psychologists, educators, psychiatrists, clergymen and theologians all stress it. It has even created a new profession—the professional marriage counselor.

Students are probably the group that need help the most, but colleges and universities have been very uncertain about their responsibility and the role they should play in premarital and marital guidance. Two functions have been developed: One is offering courses on marriage and the family; the other is providing counseling, usually through the counseling service.

The first began about the turn of the century and consisted primarily of courses on the family offered through the sociology department. These were mainly academic in nature, dealing with historical and sociological discussions of the family and its relationship to culture. Through the influence of such men as Ernest Groves and Henry Bowman these courses have become more functional and have taken into account instruction that was actually a preparation for marriage, emphasizing the nature of the marriage relationship and its involvements. Home economics departments also have offered courses in family life. These, too, have gone through a transition period, from a primary emphasis on the technology of homemaking to child care and the dynamics of family life.

Naturally, the men who taught these courses were in much demand by students for personal counseling. As they were taught both the problems and possibilities of marriage, students frequently felt the need for help. It began to be recognized that this should be a part of the university counseling service, though the number of schools that have included marriage counselors on their counseling staffs is very small. The vast majority of counselors are oriented to educational and vocational counseling, rather than to premarital guidance and family counseling.

These developments are good so far as they go. The course offerings have spread rapidly (it is estimated they are being offered on more than six hundred campuses). They are of help only to those who can work them into their schedules. This is a small percentage on the average campus. As for counseling, few campuses have sufficient counselors to do extensive family counseling. Very few campuses have counselors specifically trained for family counseling, and students do not think of the counseling service as a place to secure such help.

In many cases the pastor is in a key position. He conducts wedding services. He is identified with the home. Our concern here is with his responsibilities and his opportunities. We shall think in terms of both areas of responsibility—premarital guidance and marital counseling.

Premarital preparation.[9]   There is one sense in which preparation for marriage begins the day a person is born. A person brings his
total personality to marriage, including all of his background, attitudes, habits, ideals, likes and dislikes. All of his previous experiences, home background, and cultural surroundings influence his adjustment to marriage. There is another sense in which there is a
specific preparation for marriage. This is the preparation an individual makes when he is thinking of his own marriage and his own
home. Student groups are at the age when many are making such
plans and most of them are considering the possibility.

The tragedy is that, even yet, many people enter into marriage
with no planning or preparation at all. They attend college and professional school for from four to nine years to prepare for a vocation,
but they may enter into marriage, which is so vital for their happiness, without so much as reading a book on the subject.

At this point we would distinguish between premarital education,
premarital guidance and premarital counseling, although we recognize that for practical purposes they all overlap and no one can tell
where one leaves off and the other begins.

Premarital education may be with a group, with a couple or with
an individual. It is primarily information-centered. We have a great
deal of information about family life. The family has been the subject of more investigation and research than any area of human experience. It is unfortunate if a couple enters into marriage without
this information. If they are to have it, someone must make it available. This can be done through guided reading, discussion groups,
lectures and films. The pastor is in an ideal position to provide such
information. He already has groups in which the interest is high and
the need is very real. The subject matter for such discussions should
cover all areas of family life, its nature, its purpose, masculine and
feminine roles, physical adjustment, parenthood, the relation of vocation to the home, the method of handling quarrels and crises, relationships with in-laws, the place of religion in the home and so forth.
Much of this can be presented to a group as well as to an individual,
and, at times, more effectively. The group itself lends support. Such
groups have no magic in them. They will not turn a potentially bad
marriage into a good one, but they can be a real source of help.

Premarital guidance may also be largely information-centered, but it is an application of such matters as those just mentioned—applied and worked out by a specific couple in terms of their unique needs. It is one thing to discuss family finance in general, but another to work through a budget with one couple, both sophomores in college who want to stay in school and both of whom have time for only part-time employment. We are defining *guidance* as a form of education that involves working through specific plans and procedures.

No one knows where guidance leaves off and counseling begins. It is only for purposes of discussion that we separate them here. Everyone needs premarital education; most people need premarital guidance; some need premarital counseling. By counseling we mean that which deals basically with feelings and emotions. We are speaking now of those couples whose problems are not due to a lack of information. They need more than working through plans and procedures. They are troubled by anxiety, fear, perhaps guilt. Their problem is emotional involvement, personal adjustment. Most couples approach marriage with a certain degree of anxiety; for some it can be very severe.

One girl, a home economics major, set a date for her wedding and postponed it three times. Each time she approached the scheduled date she panicked and couldn't go through with it. She didn't need more information. She had read all the books and, as a home economics major, had taken all the courses. She needed personal counseling that would enable her to face her own problems and understand herself. She didn't need more education; she needed counseling.

A multitude of situations that can only be helped by counseling can arise on a campus. Here we include such cases as the students who want to get married and not tell their parents, or the girl whose parents disapprove and say that if she marries such and such a person they will not attend the wedding. She replies, "I love my parents, and I love Joe. If I've got to hurt somebody, I don't know who it should be." She needs counseling, probably extensive counseling.

In this category we would include interfaith marriage, with all of its ramifications, the intercultural marriage and the interracial marriage. A girl from a small rural town fell in love with a foreign student studying engineering. They prepared to be married. Her family was violently opposed. She, the foreign student and the family all sought out the pastor.

The list is endless. All such problems need someone who is patient, understanding and highly skilled to work through their involvements with them.

All these three emphases are interrelated. A good education program leads to counseling and guidance. Students who have been helped in counseling sessions profit more from group discussion and reading.

Marital counseling.[10]   It used to be that premarital counseling was the primary need on the campus. With the increasing number of married students among undergraduates and graduate students on our campuses, the pastor on the campus must think not only of his responsibilities for premarital preparation but also of his responsibilities as a family counselor.

This probably received its greatest impetus following the war when veterans returned to the campus and the trailer court became as much a part of the campus scene as the traditional dormitory. Some schools have sought to meet the problem by constructing married students' housing. Our postwar affluent society and the availability of part-time employment have encouraged the trend toward early marriages. At the same time the lengthening of education in most of the professions has increased the percentage of married students. One school of about 12,000 students usually has about 1,000 undergraduate and 1,000 graduate students each year who are married. The large coeducational schools, where housing is available, naturally have more married students than other campuses. The percentages vary from around 10 percent to 20 or 25 percent.[11]

These marriages have the same problems as any other marriage, plus some that are accentuated by the college situation. This is not a book on marriage counseling, and there is no need to duplicate what has been described very adequately in such volumes. We shall think specifically of the college situation and discuss it under three divisions, all of which carry over into each other.

First, we will discuss what we will call normal conflict. This is natural and to be expected, whether it is on the campus or off. Marriage counselors say that the tensions and adjustments of the first two years are usually the most difficult. This means that such problems should be expected to arise while these students are still in school. It means, further, that the student pastor is the one most likely to be called upon to deal with the situation.

This includes the whole range—immaturity, disillusionment, sex adjustment, conflicts with relatives, other difficulties. Some problems, if not unique to the campus, are certainly widespread there. This would include the triumvirate of lack of time, energy and money, often accompanied by a sense of disillusionment. Two people who have enjoyed being together think that if they could just get married their problems would be solved. Then they discover "two can't live as cheaply as one," that they are so busy studying, working, shopping, keeping house and so on, that they hardly have time for each other, not to mention any time for recreation and friends.

Fatigue can be a real factor affecting both marriage and study. There simply isn't enough time to do all that needs to be done. It can create misunderstanding, especially if the wife doesn't understand why her husband has to study so much and spend so many evenings in the library.

Only a small percentage have sufficient scholarship help or help from home to free them from financial worries. The usual procedure is for the wife to work and support the husband. This has definite advantages, primarily economic. It has some real cultural and personal implications. The masculine and feminine roles are reversed. Sometimes the husband is apologetic, embarrassed, almost resentful of the fact that he is dependent upon his wife. The wife, on the other hand, may become dominant or demanding, or will not understand why her husband doesn't assume more responsibility for the housework. Another problem is created if it is necessary for her to give up her educational plans to advance his.

The whole picture becomes more complicated when there are children, especially when the coming of a child necessitates changing or giving up jobs.

These situations respond well to counseling, but many of these students are in real need of someone with whom they can share their concerns.

There are also cases of severe conflict among students. This is a difference of degree, rather than of kind—but the difference is of such intensity that normal patterns are disrupted, life becomes unbearable, the students cannot study. They are in a state of constant tension. They feel that some drastic action must be taken. They may be considering divorce. The wife may have returned to her parents. They are in great confusion as to what to do.

Such situations always present people who are in the midst of great suffering, considerable embarrassment, and extreme perplexity and confusion. Their marriages and, at times, their academic and professional careers are at stake. It is a rare student who can maintain his concentration on academic matters while he is involved in so much controversy and conflict at home. There may be cases of severe conflict when the family problem is a symptom of a deeper need. The student may need to be referred for psychotherapy. The pastor works with normal people at the conscious level.

There are also couples with family problems. They are not in conflict with each other; they are faced with situations about which they don't know what to do. This may include illness, finances, the question of adopting a child, whether or not a wife should give up her educational plans, the advisability of the husband's dropping out of school to get out of debt, concern about parents, changing vocational goals—any number of problems may arise to cause a couple to seek help together. The future of their family and their home depends upon finding a solution.

The pastor, at least at present, is the person most likely to be consulted about such matters. Married students are not likely to go to the university counseling center with such problems. They very seldom go to a family service association and usually cannot afford a psychiatrist.

When the pastor does family counseling, he fulfills many functions. He begins by listening, as in all counseling. At times he is an interpreter, interpreting one to the other, and the situation to both. On occasion he is a friendly teacher, providing the students with the information they need. Sometimes he is a steadying influence, "standing by" through some difficult situation. At other times he helps them evaluate alternatives, or to work out more effective plans for a budget, a church relationship or whatever the problem may be. In deep and difficult cases he helps a person to reorganize his life and gain a new insight into his own behavior and a new understanding of the needs of others. On occasions he helps a person learn to forgive and to love. But this is not easy. It takes time, patience, and great skill, but there is no task the pastor does that is more rewarding.

If he can help students through their family difficulties while they are students, he can be quite sure he has helped a family establish family relationships that will last.

Emotional Problems

We have titled this section "Emotional Problems." It might just as well have been called "Personal Problems" or "Problems of Personality." Whatever we call it is inadequate and artificial. All problems are personal. All problems are emotional to some degree. A problem of academic failure can be very emotional in nature. A student troubled by religious doubt can feel very guilty. This is an emotion. In experience, problems and emotions cannot be dealt with separately.

We are discussing here those problems that are not basically academic or vocational. They are not premarital or religious; yet the student is having difficulty and needs help. For example, a professor discusses a girl with a pastor. She is so shy she cannot recite in class. Her written work is excellent. Her class participation is nonexistent. She secludes herself in her room, never dates, never attends any social functions. A check of her orientation tests indicate an I.Q. in the 140's. She is actually brilliant, but, paradoxically, has deep feelings of inadequacy. She has a personality problem. It's true that it has academic implications, but basically, her problem is personal and emotional.

These problems range in degree all the way from the homesickness of a freshman at the first of the semester (which may disappear as soon as he gets acquainted) to the problems of a student who is so severely disturbed that he has to be sent home or referred to a psychiatrist for treatment. Most students' problems lie somewhere on the continuum between these two extremes.

Some feel that the number at the extreme end of the scale is increasing. Drs. Gordon and Gordon, in their study of the mental health of college students, published under the title *The Blight on the Ivy*, feel there is a very real increase in emotional disorders among college students. It is their opinion that young people of college age "are having far more emotional trouble in the 1960's than they did in the 1950's."[12] They lay much of the blame on the stresses and strains of college life, the "pressures from all sides to beat the other fellow in the race, to get into college, to stay there, to rank at the top of the class, to earn a scholarship or fellowship, to head an organization, to win acceptance, to grasp the future while you are young."[13]

This does not mean that all students are disturbed. Far from it! Many students on our campuses are wholesome, sincere, well-adjusted young people. Many have personal and emotional problems. Many people in the rest of the community have personal and emotional problems, too.

What all this says to the pastor is that if he is going to work with these students, if he is going to understand them and help them, he must be aware of the nature and extent of such problems. Most of them are within the normal range. They are the type that the pastor can help. Chad Walsh, who as a professor can speak from firsthand experience, describes the modern student in these words, "He is confused, well-meaning, likeable, quietly wistful for something—he isn't quite sure what."[14] Such students need someone to talk to about their conflicts, their ambitions, their uncertainties. Such students can be helped.

Students show a wide range of needs and degrees of adjustment. The pastor will be dealing with many students who are immature. After all, some of them are only in their late teens. Many have not had the experiences that would aid their development. Maturity, however, is not a matter of chronology. Even some of the faculty members may behave immaturely at times. At the same time, some students will show a type of maturity that is beyond their years, not only in the ability to think and study difficult matters, but in adjustment to life, attitudes toward others and the ability to accept responsibility.

Many students, like the shy girl described earlier, feel inadequate and insecure. Some studies show that more than 60 percent of college students feel inferior. Such studies are misleading. They can say nothing of the degree of inferiority. After all, according to Adler, everyone feels inferior to some degree. "To be human," he said, "is to feel inferior." That college students should feel this way should not surprise us.

Students are at the stage in their development when they need to become independent of their parents, as well as other adults. This is sometimes accompaneid by misunderstanding, perhaps conflict and, not infrequently, a sense of guilt. Many students (and others as well), primarily because of childhood experiences, have difficulty with all authority figures. This brings them in conflict with professors, the administration, coaches and even some students on campus.

Ours has been called the "age of anxiety." This is almost ubiquitous. We see it everywhere. Much on a campus tends to accentuate or increase anxiety, as the Gordons point out. The pressure of classes, the fear of failure, the desire for status and recognition, the multiplicity of activities and the limited amount of time—all create anxiety. If any part of our culture is subject to stress and strain, it is a campus. Not all stress is bad. It can lead to accomplishment. When it is never relieved, when it becomes so great that it is crippling—then it can be bad.

The whole field of interpersonal relations is so vast that we can only mention it and move on. We discuss in another section the all-important task of identifying with the opposite sex, learning and accepting one's masculine or feminine role, as the case may be, finding the person with whom one can "love and be loved." Interpersonal relations also include the capacity to relate to groups, to colleagues, to superiors—resulting either in a feeling of acceptance, of belonging, with accompanying feelings of satisfaction and pleasure, or in the opposite feeling of rejection, of isolation, with the accompanying feelings of unworthiness and loneliness. The student's attitudes toward fellow students may be a mixture of hostility and appreciation, friendliness and jealousy.

The student is attempting to gain a concept of himself. Often there are wide gaps between what he is and what he would like to be, or what he feels he ought to be. Everyone needs some sense of accomplishment, some experience of success. Some students are denied this. Others have seemingly attained it but are not satisfied with their ambitions, which may be unrealistic, possibly greater than their accomplishments. A concept of one's self includes one's ideals and values. On a campus values are mixed. The moral restraints of family are often no longer present. The student is struggling to discover what is right, what is worthwhile, what is a worthy goal and purpose—or is there any at all?

This discussion could be extended indefinitely. Books like McKinney's *Counseling for Personal Adjustment* include case after case typical of every campus, such as Warren, who was isolated by his fellow students. His father was the minister of a small, rigid sect. He felt he could not take part in many activities and, consequently, felt cut off from the group and alone. Joe was finding it difficult to schedule time for study, to engage in recreation and to spend time with his wife. Betty had a great fear of failure and was in conflict with her family. Cathy was a superior girl intellectually but had been depledged by her sorority. She felt very inadequate because of her background and consistently got into trouble with people in authority. Jerry had academic problems. He was a very dependent person and had severe guilt feelings about sexual behavior. Ben was self-conscious. Sid was immature. Mary had difficulties in adjusting to her peers.[15]

Any counselor, any pastor can make his own list. The important thing is that, as Robinson points out, "These problems are numerically frequent," but they "respond readily to counseling help."[16]

Spiritual Problems

When Horace Bushnell, at the height of his great career, was asked to speak in the chapel at Yale, he chose as his subject "The Dissolving of Doubts." It is considered one of the greatest sermons in American church history. One reason for its reality was that it was, to a large extent, autobiographical. When Bushnell had been a student at Yale he went through an intense struggle with doubt himself; in fact, there was a time as a student, when, he said, "My religious life is utterly gone." It was a time when he said he experienced "agonies of mental darkness concerning God." Doubt, not faith, seemed to be more natural for him.

How he worked through from doubt to faith; how he became such

an influential figure in American Christian thought has been frequently told. The point is that he could speak to students' problems
of religious doubt because he had known the struggle.

It is commonly recognized that religious problems are common and
often accentuated on a college campus. This is an area that is considered the pastor's responsibility. He may be accepted somewhat re-
luctantly in other fields, such as academic or vocational counseling,
but here he is considered a specialist. This is as it should be.

Washington Gladden, who himself helped literally hundreds of
students, like Bushnell achieved his own faith only after a struggle
with doubt and perplexity. In his *Recollections,* he tells of his boy-
hood struggle, the great personal sense of confusion and frustration.
He described himself as a "soul in great perplexity and trouble because it could not find God." Many factors helped him work through
this problem, but he gave much of the credit to an understanding
pastor. "It was not until my eighteenth year that a clear-headed minister lifted me out of this pit, and made me see that it was perfectly
safe to trust the Heavenly Father's love for me and walk straight on
in the ways of service, waiting for no raptures, but doing His will as
best I knew it, and confiding in His friendship."[17]

Times have greatly changed since Bushnell and Gladden were students, but the struggle with doubt, confusion and perplexity still continues; if anything, the problems are more complex. Bushnell was
breaking away from the old Calvinism; Gladden lived in a time when
higher criticism and evolution disturbed many students' religious
faith. These are no longer problems, but the difficulties have been
compounded. The fact remains that the solution of the problem still
depends upon the pastor who has prepared himself to face the issues
of his day as Bushnell did in his, and to be understanding of the
problem, as the pastor was with Gladden when he was eighteen.

The modern student must find his faith in the midst of a world of
great uncertainty and confusion. He must reconcile his faith with all
the advances of modern science, technology and learning. His faith
must stand up to the attacks of many scientists, philosophers and
psychologists who see it is nothing but a neurotic illusion, an outworn
superstition, or, worse, an irrelevant factor in our modern world. This

is not easy. It is not easy for anyone, especially for a student, with his limited background.

The pastor must be prepared to work with students who represent two extremes in terms of religious background and knowledge. There are some who know very little about religion. They have only a meager background of either knowledge or experience. Some come to the campus with nothing but a record of occasional attendance at Sunday School in a class taught by a volunteer who had no Biblical or theological training. This is part of the problem. As Thornton Merriam says, speaking of students and their religious problems, "What religion they have is sometimes chiefly a body of sentiments, prejudices, and conventional behavior. . . . The scanty deposit of ideas from childhood training is insufficient capital for the intellectual market of the campus."[18]

On the other hand, the pastor must be prepared to work with students who have a great deal of information. Some have read very widely, both in class and out, from the philosophers and theologians and are as well informed (if not better) than the pastor concerning the issues that are raised in the literature. They can ask questions no man can answer. They are facing issues that have troubled philosophers and theologians for generations.

Between these two extremes are the majority of students, most of whom at times experience problems of doubt and uncertainty, which are often compounded by accompanying feelings of guilt and unworthiness.

Some students will raise questions just to test the pastor. It is an interesting and rather ancient student tradition. They do the same with professors on the campus. In such a contest, if it is permitted to become one, the pastor is likely to lose. Any capable student can raise questions with which wise men have been grappling for years. There may be some value in such encounters, but it should be recognized that little is accomplished by religious argument; such sparring is not counseling. We are thinking here of the students who have a real concern, are genuinely troubled by religious questions and have a sincere desire to know and understand.

There are some students whose religious problems may be incidental to, or symptoms of, their main problems. A girl went to the university pastor, saying, "I don't believe in God anymore." She ostensibly intended to discuss her doubts. In the course of the conversation she said, "Now about my mother. . . ." It turned out that another problem was causing her more concern than her doubt. Once her relationship with her mother was worked through, her doubts no longer troubled her.

This does not mean that all theological problems are psychological or emotional in origin. It does mean that many are, and the wise pastor will distinguish between them and decide which needs the major attention.

There are other cases in which the religious problem is interrelated to some other problem. This is especially true in interfaith marriage. When a Protestant student falls in love with a Catholic or a Jewish student—as the case may be—and they discuss it with the pastor, they not only must face all other matters pertaining to marriage, but each must evaluate and ponder his own religious convictions and religious affiliations as well. You cannot deal with the marriage situation without considering whether or not one gives up his church relationship. They are all interrelated.

For some, religion itself is the major cause for concern. It may be the first time the student has heard the religious beliefs of his family and home church challenged or, in some cases, opposed or ridiculed. It is quite possible, especially if he comes from a small community, that he may never have come in contact with religious positions other than his own. This may take place in a classroom where the professor presents ideas that are incompatible with those the student has previously learned in Sunday School and church; it may be in a dormitory bull session, where the religious convictions he has always felt were generally accepted are subject to ridicule. Furthermore, his background has provided him with no arguments to offer in return.

It is not easy to maintain faith on a college campus, or any other place, for that matter. Daniel Jenkins, in his little book in the Layman's Theological Library, titled *Believing in God*, said, "One of the most misleading assumptions that is made about belief in God is that there ever was a time when men found it really easy."[19]

This is especially true for the student. Here he is, in the midst of a center of learning, with the responsibility of relating his religious ideas to all the findings of modern science, to all the confusing (and at times contradictory) findings of psychology, philosophy, anthropology, sociology, history and so on. This is not easy for the theologian. No wonder the student gets confused.

The whole atmosphere of the campus complicates the problem both for the student and the pastor. On many campuses the pastor is working in an environment that is not predominantly religious, at least in the traditional sense. Merrimon Cuninggim, after conducting a survey of expressions of religion on the campus, said, "The prevailing atmosphere of higher education today is secular . . . and the total impact upon the majority of students is, if not anti-, at least non-religious."[20] This is probably as true of church-related campuses as of any others. This is not to say there is no religion present, nor is it to ignore the fact that many professors are very devout, active churchmen. We have stressed this elsewhere in this volume. It is simply to recognize the fact that conditions have changed in higher education. As Dr. Henry Pitney Van Dusen points out in his book *God in Education,* religion once was the "keystone of the educational arch"; now, he says, "it is one stone among many," and many people do not see a place for it in the general structure.[21]

The place of religion in higher education is a subject for another discussion. It is mentioned in a book on student counseling in order to recognize the fact that the student lives in an environment in which religion is not a major factor, in which values and general patterns are influenced largely by a secular, materialistic, achievement- and success-minded culture. The student who is idealistic and spiritually sensitive may not feel at home. The student who is having difficulty with his religious beliefs may find more to encourage his doubts than to support his faith.

We do not know how many students are troubled by doubt. We would guess that all of them are, at some time or another and at least to some degree. Several years ago the Y.M.C.A. conducted a survey of approximately 9,000 young people of college age. It was published under the title *The Religious Beliefs of Youth.*[22] The findings revealed that only 16 percent had a clear and meaningful conception of God. Seventy-seven percent believed in God but were torn by varying degrees of doubt and uncertainty. Seven percent were openly agnostic or atheistic. Whether or not these percentages apply on every campus we do not know.

It is known that the number is large, and that for many it is a cause for considerable anxiety and distress. Doubt leaves one with a feeling of uncertainty, with a sense of being cut off from God—left in a meaningless universe. At times it is complicated by a feeling of guilt. It is also often accompanied by a feeling of estrangement from one's family and traditional background. Here is a student who tells of his religious background and of his rather intense struggle with doubt. When asked if he had discussed this at home, he said, "Oh, no, I wouldn't dare let my family or my pastor know some of the things I think or feel."

There is literally no limit to the kinds of questions and problems a student may raise. They may be questions engendered by studies that have to do with beliefs and practices. They may relate to current events, such as the stand of the church on social issues. Many students of real religious conviction are concerned about the seeming irrelevance of the church. The problem may arise from interpretations of Scripture, an understanding of the creeds or an attempt to understand Augustine or Luther. It may grow out of the student's reading of contemporary theologians or novelists. It may have to do with denominational differences, religious traditions or moral customs. It may be a general dissatisfaction with his own religious experience as such, coupled with a genuine desire to understand and experience some value from worship and private prayer. It may be a deep inner personal struggle with life's ultimate loyalties and commitments. Students are asking profound questions about life's deepest meaning and their own ultimate concerns.

These are questions and problems that the pastor must be prepared to face. Here the pastor must go beyond the psychologist or the counselor. As Merriam points out, "It is the churches . . . among all the institutions of society, which persistently are concerned with the problem of ultimate meanings and loyalties and which convey from generation to generation the result of man's attempts to find a satisfactory answer."[23]

This is not easy. There is no "method" or technique by which it can be done. It means that the pastor must be thoroughly trained in counseling. He must realize it is not his function to rush in, to be-come a defender of the faith, to preach or argue. He provides in-formation when information is needed. At times he listens as the student expresses his uncertainty and concern. At all times he pro-vides the atmosphere in which the student can face any problem or any concern without fear of censure or blame.

We do not claim that the pastor has answers for all the student's questions. No man is wise enough for that. It *is* expected that the pastor be well-informed and acquainted with the issues. At times he may become the friendly teacher, pointing out errors when they occur, providing information when it is needed—but always standing by the student in his search.

The pastor knows that doubt can be a stepping-stone to faith. The Bible is replete with examples. We quote Habbakuk in our worship services, "The Lord is in His Holy temple," but Habbakuk also said, "O Lord, how long shall I cry unto Thee and Thou wilt not hear." The Psalms are filled with expressions of faith, but they also say, "Wilt Thou forget me forever?" "How long wilt Thou hide Thy face from me?" Paul said, ". . . now we see through a glass darkly." Even Luther said, "Sometimes I believe and sometimes I doubt."

The pastor maintains this perspective. He stands by the student in his struggle with doubt and in his search for meaning until, like Bushnell and Gladden, he can work from doubt to faith. This might well be the most important thing the student does while on the campus.

CHAPTER TWO

SPECIAL GROUPS Of STUDENTS

Gifted Students

Perhaps the most strategic group on the campus is composed of the gifted students; but we should define our terms. In one sense, nearly all college students are gifted. The very fact that they have been admitted to college indicates a fairly high level of intelligence, especially if they have survived the freshman year.

By gifted, we mean the *very gifted*. We are talking about the gifted among the gifted. Unfortunately many gifted young people do not go to college. In Lewis M. Terman's group of gifted children, on which he based his famous study, 15 percent never entered college, 30 percent did not graduate. In Kansas in 1955, only 61 percent of the valedictorians and salutatorians in high school graduating classes continued their education.[1] This is cause for great concern but is another story. Our concern here is with the gifted students who are on our campuses. If we use Terman's classification, we are talking about the top 1 percent of the population, or those who have an I.Q. level of 130 and above. Of course, there are students who will register an I.Q. of 150 and above. This places them in the top tenth of the top 1 percent.

Actually, the I.Q. identifies those students who have a high level of abstract and verbal intelligence. The kind of students who score high on intelligence tests (which might better be termed "scholastic aptitude tests") can do abstract reasoning well. They can do relational thinking. They have high verbal and mathematical skill. A mental ability test will not locate the student who is gifted in such areas as music or art or social leadership. A person with a high I.Q. may or may not have talents in such areas.

If we want to think in terms of definitions rather than scores, the National Education Association defines giftedness as "a high order of ability to handle ideas, to produce creatively, and to demonstrate social leadership." Dr. Paul Witty, of Northwestern University, who is recognized as one of the foremost authorities in this field, describes a gifted person as "one whose performance in a potentially valuable line of human activity is consistently remarkable."[2] DeHaan and Havighurst, in their book *Educating Gifted Children,* refer to the gifted person as one "who is superior in some ability that can make him an outstanding contributor to the welfare of, and quality of living in, society."[3]

We shall return to this idea of their contribution to society in a moment, but first, as counselors, we must recognize the fact that the gifted, too, have problems. Douglas Thom, the psychiatrist, points out that "very little recognition has been given to the fact that extremely high intelligence is as far from normal as is mental deficiency and that it creates problems of its own that may be as acute . . . as the problems of inferior intelligence."[4] We do not have the mentally deficient on our campuses but we do have those whose intelligence is supremely high. Edith Stedman, in a research project on Personnel Programs for Gifted Students in Colleges and Universities, emphasizes the same idea as Dr. Thom. "The problems of superior students," she found, "are often undetected and even neglected."[5] There has been a vast amount of literature on counseling and guidance in recent years, but very little has been written on the counseling and guidance of gifted students.

In spite of the extensive and conclusive research of such men and women as Terman, Hollingworth, Witty, Havighurst and others, many misconceptions of the very gifted still exist. Even some educators and pastors are not informed and are still influenced by old stereotypes, superstitions and misinformation. There is no common pattern for the gifted. On the contrary, gifted students show variation and are more likely to differ from each other than they are to be similar.

Research has shown quite conclusively that as a group they do not suffer from compensating inferiorities, eccentricities or poor adjustment; in fact, taken as a whole, the opposite is true. They are stronger physically, less likely to suffer emotional breakdowns, less likely to become involved in immoral or delinquent behavior. They invariably have a wide margin of interests, are extremely versatile and are more likely to achieve academic and professional success.

This does not mean they do not have problems. They do. Their very giftedness creates some of them. The brilliant student has the same emotional needs as any other student. He, too, needs acceptance, affection, a sense of belonging. His great capacities, his superiority over others (including professors at times) may deprive him of some of these normal needs and satisfactions. The result is that often we find the paradoxical situation of a very superior person feeling very inferior.

The very gifted person often finds it difficult to find agreeable companionship, with the result that he feels lonely, isolated, different and insecure. This problem began for him long before he reached the campus. If he is in the top 1 percent he may have been aware of his differences by the time he was eight or nine years old. After all, if he had an I.Q. of 130 when he was nine, he had a mental age of twelve. This meant that he had different interests, different abilities, a different vocabulary. While he may have been far in advance of his peer group intellectually, he was not advanced physically and socially. Such children are often ostracized by their playmates, misunderstood by their teachers and exploited by their parents.

It is no wonder that Terman said, "Extreme precocity unavoidably complicates the problem of social adjustment."[6] Some may hide their intellectual differences in order to gain acceptance by the group. Some may seek recognition for their superiority. Others may develop attitudes of intolerance and disdain for those less endowed. Some may withdraw within themselves or seek satisfaction in intellectual pursuits. At any rate, difficult interpersonal relationships and feelings of loneliness and isolation may result.

The campus should provide an outlet for many such young people. Here they are more likely to find others of equal capacity. Here they should find their intellectual abilities challenged. Gifted students can have academic difficulties, however. This, too, is usually due to earlier experiences. Because of his superiority over his age group the student may have developed attitudes of overconfidence, idleness or laziness. Now confronted with stiffer competition and more demands, he may not have either the attitudes or study habits to cope with the situation. As Freehill emphasizes, "Superior intelligence does not make effective work habits less desirable."[7] To quote Terman once more, "The exceptionally bright student who is kept with his age group finds little to challenge his intelligence and all too often develops habits of laziness that can wreck his college career."[8]

The most prevalent problem academically is not that the gifted student will fail, but that he will fail to live up to his full potential. He is able to maintain a satisfactory scholastic level with a minimum of effort and efficiency and thus operates far below his possibilities. This means he does not find personal satisfaction or make the contribution of which he is capable. Gifted students do have intellectual needs that are not often met without planning and guidance. Gifted students will not gravitate to their appropriate educational level by chance any more than they will develop good study habits by chance. Some will; others could benefit greatly from guidance.

The gifted student often has difficulty in finding satisfactory outlets for his talents. On most campuses the pace is geared to the average student—as, no doubt, it should be. For the gifted student, this is too easy. Some schools are recognizing this fact and attempting to provide opportunities that overcome it. Some admit younger students, even, in some cases, those without high school diplomas. Many colleges have developed honors programs through which students whose capabilities permit can do advanced reading, conduct special research and share in special seminar discussions.

The gifted student can do so many things well that even the choice of a major is difficult. This problem is further complicated by the tremendous competition for brains in America, which causes many people to put pressure on the gifted student to enter certain fields— with little regard for *his* interests and desires. This is recruitment and not guidance.

Achievement by the gifted—and others, for that matter—is closely related to motivation and to vocational goals.

The problem of choosing a vocation is even more difficult than choosing a major; in fact, the two cannot be separated. The gifted student has a wide range from which to choose. Because he can do so many things well, he faces a difficulty of decision the average person does not face at all. He is fully aware that the choice involves a wide diversity of experiences; in fact, it is a choice of different ways of life, as we stress in the section on vocational guidance. A study of Phi Beta Kappa members and the problems on which they sought counseling revealed that this was the problem most frequently mentioned.[9]

It is a real misfortune that so many gifted persons find themselves in vocations that do not require their full potential. This is a great loss to society and to the student as well. They never gain the sense of self-fulfillment that comes with work that offers a real challenge and demands their best.

The pastor's primary concern with all students is their religious growth and development. Here again the gifted student may have something of a problem because of his very giftedness. All students have their questions and doubts, at least most students do. For the gifted student these questions are likely to be more complex and profound than they are for the average student. He may be asking questions at a deeper level than the pastor himself has asked. Because of his high level of intelligence and wide range of reading, he frequently finds it difficult to find someone who can understand the implications of the questions he is raising, let alone provide the answers. After all, he raises questions the wisest philosophers and theologians have been wrestling with for generations. He is not satisfied with clichés, cheap reassurance or inadequate thinking. He is grappling with real issues.

In all this discussion one aspect has predominated—the great potential of the gifted student. He is a five-talent person with a great contribution that should be made. All too often these students fail to have the sense of responsibility for the use of their talents. It is the pastor's task not only to help them solve their problems but to create a sense of dedication and commitment. This is a service both to the student and to society.

There are some students who sense this. Some seek counseling not because they are disturbed or depressed but because they have an awareness of what life ought to mean and what they ought to do, but are aware that they have not attained it as yet. As Dr. Francis Robinson puts it, they are conscious that "the normal is not good enough." This is what he calls counseling for "high-level skills of adjustment."[10] It is not counseling that deals with a so-called problem but counseling that helps a student who is living on an average level to obtain a much higher level of adjustment and effectiveness.

Although we have stressed the fact that the gifted students do have problems, there is a compensating factor. They also have a greater capacity to solve their problems. They have a greater capacity for self-diagnosis. They come to insights more quickly and can deal with stress and tension more effectively than others. Thom's study of gifted children found that those of high intelligence were less likely to retain their problems than were those of lower intelligence.[11]

Gifted students are able to understand the counseling process and cooperate with it, and this says something about counseling procedures. The permissive approach to counseling has values for all students but especially for the very gifted. His problems are so complex, his alternatives are so many, his reasoning capacity is so profound that he must reach his own decisions and come to his own insights. No one can do it for him. An understanding pastor (even though he may not be able to match the student's brilliance) can render a great service by providing the atmosphere wherein these problems and decisions can be thought through, free from emotion and pressure.

The pastor has another service to offer the gifted student. Intelligence alone is not enough, either for success or happiness. Even the most gifted also need persistence, motivation, understanding, acceptance, love, purpose and faith. These are the things in which the pastor should be a specialist. These are high-level skills of a spiritual nature that everyone needs.

Foreign Students

There is a large group of foreign students on our campuses. According to the Institute of International Education they number over 48,000.[12] More than half of them are in undergraduate programs. About three-fourths of them are men. They represent more than one hundred and fifty countries and are to be found on more than 1,100 campuses.[13] On some campuses they are found in great numbers.

The University of California has almost 2,000; New York University, more than 1,500. Several schools have as many as 1,000. In the large schools that attract many foreign students, the ratio of foreign to American students is about 1 to 25. In smaller liberal arts schools the ratio may be 1 to 100 or more.[14]

These students are often carefully selected. They may be very brilliant. Many will obtain key positions of leadership and occupy places of real influence in national and international affairs. For this reason alone they deserve careful consideration. From the standpoint of this study they are of concern because they are persons and, as persons, have needs and problems which can be helped and alleviated through counseling.

There is no such thing as *the* foreign student. As in all other areas of human behavior, each must be seen in his own light. There are national and cultural patterns, but there is also great variation within national and cultural groups.

Their motives (in contrast to some American students) are primarily educational. They are here to gain knowledge and training. As students they have the same problems, academic and vocational, that other students have, but also some that are unique and some that are accentuated because they are foreign students.

Some of the foreign student's problems arise before he even enters the country. These include preliminary negotiations, admission to the university, financial arrangements, the securing of passports and so forth. While these details may have an important bearing on the student's experience, most are handled by the university personnel, and unless a church group is sponsoring the foreign student, are not the concern of the pastor.

Common to all foreign students is the fact that they are away from home, many for the first time. Homesickness, loneliness and worry about family are natural and to be expected. Sometimes this can be alleviated by simple friendship; sometimes it is so severe as to cause actual illness and hamper or even cut short a student's educational plans.

This problem is especially likely to arise at such times as vacations and holidays like Christmas, Thanksgiving and Easter, when other students desert the campus in large numbers. The dormitories are empty or closed. Here again a pastor or a church group can render a service. If it is a small campus where only a few foreign students are present, arrangements for their entertainment may not be too difficult. On campuses where there are a great number, such provisions present something of a problem.

Housing itself may be an important factor, especially where dormitory facilities are limited and where color is a problem. So important is this that Blegen and Cooper say, "The student's reactions to his new life may be influenced to a greater extent by his housing accommodations than by any other single factor."[15]

The language barrier is an obvious problem. For students who have a good grasp of English, this creates no disadvantage. Others experience a real strain as they try to keep up with assignments but read very slowly and only catch a portion of lectures or class discussion. This creates a dilemma for the professor as well. Does he have time to give the student extra attention? Does he make allowances for language difficulties in making out grades? If he does, is it fair to American students? Such problems are not all problems of learning. They create emotional problems as well, feelings of inadequacy, frustration and futility.

All of this creates a problem in counseling as well. Counseling is based on communication. The student must feel he is being heard and understood. We remember very vividly attempting to counsel a student who had a very limited use of English. He was under some stress, and it was difficult to get many words and even sentences that he spoke. To interrupt the flow of language, to ask such a student to repeat, only adds to the frustration; yet, if the counselor isn't sure of what is being said, he is in no position to understand.

Not only the foreign students' language is different, but their cultural patterns are different. They are "strangers in an unfamiliar culture."[16] The foreign student must become acquainted with different customs, different eating habits, different racial attitudes, different traffic laws and regulations—the list is endless. The foreign student finds himself in a culture different from his own—and often different from the one he expected. Advance publicity may have misled him about America and campus life. Different attitudes toward work, the family and the nation are all confusing.

Different cultural patterns also are influential in the counseling process. Most pastors and counselors are trained in a counseling philosophy and technique that are uniquely applicable to a democratic society. In a course in counseling techniques, an Oriental student from a paternalistic culture could not grasp the permissive philosophy of Carl Rogers at all. "This doesn't make sense," he protested continuously. "In my country we are supposed to tell the people what to do." Obviously, students from such a background find it difficult to understand the permissive type of counseling that is so characteristic of most American counselors.

Some problems of foreign students have to do with very practical matters. Forrest J. Moore, Foreign Student Advisor at the University of Minnesota, says if you are going to list foreign students' problems in the order of frequency, financial problems would be number one.[17] They often lack information about what is needed; they use more for travel than they had expected; they have unexpected expenses because of illness—these and other situations can create financial problems that cause much uncertainty and concern. If one does have a serious illness, an understanding doctor can be of great help. Again, this is a time when attention, friendship and understanding are invaluable.

Many of these students are not Christian. For most of them this is their first contact with Christianity or the organized expression of it in the church. This raises many questions, and, for someone who has been influenced by missionaries, some disillusionment. This is a pastor's particular responsibility. The students may come to discuss it with him, or they may not. But, if they do, he is both a counselor and an interpreter of the faith. He is a missionary in America.

Dr. Mueller says that the counselor with foreign students should realize that the foreign student goes through four "recognizable stages." These often overlap, and lines of separation cannot be sharply drawn; nevertheless, there are four stages which present different kinds of problems. First is the spectator stage. In this stage all is new, exciting, at times frustrating. Language barriers may be quite acute; the student is under tension but not threatened too much. The second stage is called the adaptive stage. In this stage he enters into his tasks. It is necessary for him to adapt to and participate in American programs and American culture. Here he encounters many surprises, experiences, resistance within himself; he may experience some stress as a result. The third stage is called the "coming to terms" stage. Here he comes to terms with his new environment. He weighs and re-evaluates his own goals and convictions. He conforms or refuses to, depending on his personality. The final stage is the predepartive stage. Now he sees the new culture and his whole experience in it from a new perspective. He also must re-evaluate his own country and his own culture in the light of his experience in America.[18] There may be another stage after he returns to his own country and faces the necessity of readjusting there, but there is nothing the pastor can do about that except to prepare him for it.

It is obvious, from the previous discussion, that any campus that has a large concentration of such students should have a counselor, or advisor, to foreign students who is familiar with their needs, who is thoroughly acquainted with the legal technicalities relative to their entrance and stay in the country and who is sensitive to their problems. The pastor should know this person and work with him when foreign students come to him for counseling. The two men, each working in his own specialty, can greatly help each other. On small campuses, where there is no foreign student advisor, a chaplain or pastor may, of necessity, assume some of these responsibilities himself.

We have been talking of foreign students in general, but it should be recognized that in counseling each must be seen as an individual. There is probably wider variation among foreign students than among any other group. There are wide cultural and racial differences. Students from Canada are quite different from those from Mexico, who, in turn, have different racial attitudes from those held by students from Africa, the Orient or northern Europe. There are also differences within the same cultural groups. Five students from Germany may present five different personality patterns and experience different kinds of problems in the course of their educational experiences.

These different cultural patterns, as mentioned earlier in the case of the Oriental student in the counseling course, do not always lend themselves to counseling, at least to the kind of counseling most pastors and counselors have been trained to do. If they come from backgrounds where government and family groups have dictated their behavior, they don't know how to react to a permissive type of relationship. Their concept of counseling may be quite different from the counselor's. Their attitude may be expressed thus: "You are the counselor. You can solve my problem. Tell me what to do."

For this reason, Mueller suggests that the counselor to foreign students would do well "to forget most of his previous experiences and many of the usual techniques of counseling. He has a new kind of personality to learn."[19]

Recognizing all of these factors, we must realize that the foreign student, like anyone else, responds to friendship, understanding and acceptance. It is often the pastor's privilege to provide such a relationship, and thus make a real contribution to the educational experience and the personal life of an individual who is far away from home and, incidentally, to make no small contribution to world attitudes of friendship and understanding.

Graduate Students

It is no doubt true that most of a pastor's time will be spent with undergraduates, but it should also be recognized that a large number of graduate students are on many of our campuses, that the number is increasing and that they, too, have needs. It is difficult to say how many graduate students there really are. Many are studying part-time; some, like teachers, just take work during the summers; many are registered only for theses. A general, and perhaps conservative, estimate is that more than 250,000 students are registered for graduate degrees. About two-thirds of these are in their first year of graduate study. About half of them are on a doctoral program.[20]

These are rather large figures when one considers that graduate education is relatively new in the United States. The first earned Ph.D. in America was granted by Yale University in 1861. Educational historians usually date the beginning of graduate work in this country at the time of the establishment of Johns Hopkins University in 1876. This was less than a century ago. Since then graduate programs have undergone many changes; they are still in a process of development, and have grown very rapidly, especially since World War II. Graduate education used to be centered in the East. In the 1930's, five schools awarded one-half of all Ph.D. degrees. These were Columbia, Chicago, Harvard, Johns Hopkins and Yale. In the 1950's the five schools that awarded the largest number of Ph.D.'s were Columbia, Wisconsin, California, Harvard and Illinois, but they granted degrees to fewer than one-fourth of the total.[21]

In some fields graduate work, even the Ph.D., is almost a prerequisite for employment or advancement; in fact, the doctorate has become so common in some areas that there is now a trend for post-doctoral programs. Some schools have even established programs for postdoctoral work and advanced research. Graduate schools are recognized as the major home for research in all fields and the source of most of our college-level teachers and many professional workers.

A discussion on counseling graduate students begins at the under-graduate level, when the student is facing the decision as to whether or not to do graduate work. This can be at any time but most frequently occurs during the junior or senior year in college. It begins with questions in the student's mind. One of the most common is: Can I make it? Also he asks himself or his counselor: Is it worth it? How can I afford it? How long will it take? Of what value will it be? Are scholarships available? What are the best schools? Will I be admitted? What about lanugages? Is one school as good as another? Do I want to delay marriage and a family? Is it necessary in my field?

These important questions should be considered carefully. A graduate program requires too much of an investment of time, effort, money and emotional involvement to be undertaken without a careful consideration of all of the implications.

Of those who do continue for graduate work, only about half go full-time. The others work a program around their job of teaching, or whatever it might be. The majority of graduate students are married. Of those who receive doctorates in 1957, half were married when they began their work and three-fourths were married by the time they had completed it.

While graduate programs vary by fields and by schools, one common characteristic is that they all require research. As one faculty member said, "The business of the graduate faculty member is research."[22] This influences the admission polices. As Berelson points out, they admit students "primarily or exclusively on the basis of one criterion—intellectual capacity."[23] Naturally some of them have emotional problems.

When we combine the factors mentioned in these last few paragraphs (the fact that many are attempting two tasks—the pursuit of a vocation and an advanced degree, that the majority are married and have assumed family responsibilities, an admissions policy which considers only intellectual capacity and a faculty interested primarily in research) and add to these the fact that graduate study is characterized by intense competition and high-level expectations and is a long and drawn-out process . . . the need for counseling is obvious.

Most graduate schools, however, do not conceive of counseling as one of their primary responsibilities. The graduate student is selected because of his ability and is presumed to have maturity and stability—a big assumption, to be sure—but he is not expected to require guidance like that needed by the undergraduate. To quote Ness again, in his *Guide to Graduate Study*, "Whereas a majority of undergraduate colleges maintain fairly extensive counseling facilities, the graduate student will find a minimum of guidance."[24]

Fortunately, there are exceptions. There are faculty members who are interested in students as persons and are willing to help them with decisions and so forth. In the main, the faculty of a graduate school is made up of specialists, highly trained in their own areas. They do not have the time or the training or the inclination to do extensive counseling; in fact, in some large universities it is necessary to make an appointment weeks in advance even to get into a professor's office.

That graduate students are as likely to have problems as undergraduates is to say the obvious. In some ways, they are more mature, but, also, they are subject to more pressures. As one graduate student said, "Uncertainty seems to be the greatest problem for the new graduate student. Anxiety, often from purely imaginary sources, plagues him about courses, grades, requirements, the difficulty of the oral examination, the bugaboo of the thesis, and so forth."[25]

Just as the transition from high school to college demanded more initiative and self-direction, so the move from college to graduate study demands greater effort and discipline; in fact, the student must accept almost complete responsibility for his own progress. He is confronted with a continuous series of challenges—courses, language tests, orals and, of course, the dissertation. This last seemingly causes more concern than any other. Perhaps more students do not complete their degrees because of the dissertation than for any other reason. Some schools speak of the ABD degree, All But Dissertation.[26]

This, it would seem, is a place where the pastor, or the university pastor, or the chaplain, as the case may be, has a real opportunity. He will only be able to exercise it if he gets to know these students personally. They, with a few exceptions, will not be in his program for students.

This last factor is one which the pastor might well consider. There is almost no provision made for the social life of the graduate student. He does not feel at home in the undergraduate social functions. He has limited leisure time and usually limited funds, but he and his family would benefit from social activities with others with whom they could share interests and concerns. More than most people, he needs the church to draw him into relaxing, meaningful, social activities, because of high tension and fatigue due to long hours bent over books and typewriter.

Graduate students also have high ethical ideals. They are grappling with vital issues. They welcome an opportunity to discuss the theological implications of their vocational commitment, the meaning of their study and research. Out of such groups and such contacts may grow opportunities for personal counseling of a very significant nature.

Pretheological and Seminary Students

Two groups of students are of major concern to the pastor because of his unique relationship to them. These are the pretheological students on our undergraduate campuses and the seminary students in our graduate theological schools. These two groups are different in some respects, very similar in others.

These students are preparing themselves for a rather wide diversity of fields of service commonly referred to as the church vocations.

These include the pastorate; the associate or assistant pastorate; the mission field, with all of its many expressions; Christian education; youth work; the ministry to students; the institutional chaplaincy; the military chaplaincy; religious radio and television; religious journalism and so forth.

The pastor has both an interest in and a major responsibility for these candidates for church vocations. He may have recruited a few and may have a personal relationship and involvement with them. Others may have come to him to discuss their decision. There are exceptions, but the candidate for the ministry is more likely to seek the counsel of a pastor than of professionally trained counselor. Moreover, school and vocational counselors are likely to solicit his aid with such students. Professional counselors are very skeptical about pastors doing vocational guidance, and rightfully so; yet at this point they want him to be a specialist. They want the pastor to refer vocational problems to them; they want to refer candidates for church vocations to him.

There are some obvious reasons why this is so. The religious scene in America is so complex that no counselor can be acquainted with all of it. The many denominations—each with its own schools, its own requirements for ordination, its own standards for qualification, its own system of placement, its own organization of mission work, its own concept of the ministry, its nature and its call—present a picture too complex and too confusing for a vocational counselor to grasp.

It is further complicated by the concept of the "call." A person decides "to go into" law, medicine or education. He is "called" into the ministry. Again there is great diversity not only between denominations but within one denomination as to what constitutes a call. We do not have the time to discuss either the theology or the psychology of the "call" here. All we can do is to point out that this is an area in which the pastor must have some understanding and be able to work effectively, because both the student and the university counselors turn to him at this point.

It is a most significant area of responsibility. In some ways it is one of the most important areas in which a pastor can work. The welfare of the individual is at stake, first of all. Anyone considering the high calling of the Christian ministry deserves all the guidance and help he can get. His whole future is involved. Also the future of the church is involved. It is no reflection on the laity to say that the future of the church is dependent to a large extent on the quality and dedication of its leadership.

This is no small group of which we are speaking. The Niebuhr, Gustafson and Williams report, which appeared in 1957, estimated that approximately 24,000 students are in our seminaries, or one for every 2,375 church members.[27] This does not include undergraduates who are engaged in preseminary studies.

Pretheological students. Pretheological students are found on all of our campuses. More tend to be concentrated on church-related campuses, but many are found on large state university campuses; in fact, there seems to be a trend in this direction. On a large campus (or small one, too, for that matter) there may be a feeling of isolation. The preministerial candidate is lost in a host of engineers, lawyers, teachers and so on. He may be hesitant to discuss his vocational aspirations with other students, possibly even to admit them. Here the university pastor can do much by bringing such students together for fellowship and discussion of mutual problems. Such group sessions will often lead to some very fruitful individual counseling.

Pretheological students can be divided into two broad groups. The first group consists of those students who have already decided on the ministry.[28] The student in this group may question his decision at times, to be sure, but he has declared his purpose; he knows the general direction in which he wants to go. He faces certain academic questions, such as how to plan a program of study which will provide the best background for seminary. Should he major in religion or one of the social sciences? How important are Greek and Hebrew? Should he preach while he is still an undergraduate? What factors should be considered in the selection of a seminary.

Another group is quite undecided. This group is a part of that vast segment of our college population whose members don't know what they want to do. They may have started on another major but aren't satisfied with it and wonder if they want to change. They have strong leanings toward the ministry, but also feel quite hesitant and uncertain. Some students are in conflict with their parents who do not share in, or understand, their desire to go into the ministry. Some have deep feelings of unworthiness, doubt and guilt. Some may question their ability to succeed either in seminary or in a church. Others wonder about the "call." They may have strong motivations for Christian service but have never experienced anything that corresponds to a "call" as they have heard it described, or as it may be expected in their own denominational groups. Some may have invested considerable time and money in another field and feel this would all be wasted. Some have deep religious commitments but seriously question whether one can serve in the church as it is constituted today and as it is so much a part of our culture. Some have physical or emotional handicaps. Some may have speech defects and wonder if they can serve. The list could be extended. It is obvious that such problems can only be worked through in a counseling session—and the person most qualified to do it is the pastor who has some training as a counselor. It is also obvious that this is not counseling that can be done on any superficial level. These are young people making decisions that will affect their whole lives; they are facing issues that have to do with ultimates.

Occasionally in such counseling the pastor feels the student is not qualified for the ministry. This is a most delicate situation. In the first place, who is capable of predicting what a person will be ten years from now, or after thorough training? Who is wise enough to know whether or not handicaps are alterable or unalterable? Can a speech defect be corrected? Can an overly shy person gain self-confidence with counseling? Can the person guilty of immoral behavior really be converted and change sufficiently to lead others? If it is necessary to discourage a student, how can he be rerouted so that he will not lose his self-respect? How can he still utilize his religious motives so he can render a service and be a better layman?

Counseling for church vocations is not dissimilar from counseling for other vocations; that is, it must depend on a thorough knowledge of the individual and a thorough knowledge of the task.

Here again the pastor has a unique opportunity and responsibility. The student can go to the counseling center and get information about medicine, or law or social work. Professional counselors are not as well informed about the ministry and its many expressions. The fact is that many students make a decision for the ministry without really understanding what it involves at all. Others do not consider the ministry because they have a misconception of its true nature. We recall one student who went into social work because he wanted to help people. When asked if he had considered the ministry, he said, "No, because they mainly get up and talk." The whole pastoral concept of the ministry was unfamiliar to him, though he had been raised in the church. Here again, the pastor is the one who has such information at his fingertips and should be a real help to students and, incidentally, to the professional counselors as well.

Seminary students. There are eighty-eight seminaries that are members of the American Association of Theological Schools and forty others that are affiliated with it. Some of these are on larger campuses, as one school in a university, such as Yale, Harvard and Texas Christian University. Others are separate institutions, consisting of a seminary alone, such as Colgate-Rochester Divinity School, College of the Bible and Pacific School of Religion. Here are found the 24,000 plus students mentioned above. Most of them are men, though not all. Many women are preparing for religious education, the mission field and so forth. A majority of these students are married.

Theological students go to seminary for a great variety of reasons. Many motivations lead a person to seminary, as anyone knows who has administered the Theological School Inventory (TSI) to groups of incoming students. Results of studies on the TSI show differences among seminaries, among denominations and within a seminary. Some students are strongly motivated to gain the approval of others; some are not. Some have great intellectual curiosity about things religious; others do not. Some have a passion to preach; with others this is quite low. Some have a strong desire to correct the evils of society; with others this is almost nonexistent. Some have a great personal concern for individuals; others score very low on this scale.

The Niebuhr report, mentioned earlier, lists ten different groups or types of persons found on our seminary campuses. We are indebted to this list, as anyone familiar with it can see, but we have created our own and have come up with a larger number.[29] As in all such lists, it is highly artificial. Many of these areas overlap. No student is exclusively in one area or the other. Yet, for purposes of discussion, these categories are at least suggestive.

There is the student who has been persuaded by a well-meaning parent, pastor or friend that this is what he ought to do. Maybe it is. Some students find out that it is what they really want to do. On the other hand, there are those who have been pressured into the ministry. They never really had a chance to make a choice for themselves. It is no wonder that at times they feel lost, a bit hostile and perhaps drop out of seminary. This group will score high on the "A" score of the TSI. Some do become good ministers; others continue but never have a sense of commitment. Some leave the ministry.

Some seminary students are seeking, either consciously or unconsciously, to save their own souls. Suffering from deep feelings of guilt, anxiety or estrangement, they turn to religion as a way of healing and peace. This is not necessarily bad, providing it is not crippling and providing the student can work through his difficulties and gain some self-understanding. Many men go into psychotherapy or social work for the same reasons. Once these conflicts have been resolved, the individual can become more useful than he would have been otherwise.

An intense interest in things religious motivates some students to enter the seminary. They like to ask the questions: Whence? Whither? and Why? They have great intellectual curiosity. They would score high on the "I" score of the TSI. They are the scholars of the future. They must take basic courses but often get impatient with the so-called "practical" courses and, at times, with students and professors as well. They often are enamored with the idea of securing a Ph.D. in religion. Some should continue and acquire it, by all means, but some lack the capacity for further studies and may need to learn to be content with some of the practical matters of the parish.

Other students in seminary have already been active in religious work. They have been active in student fellowships, in youth camps and conferences; they may have participated in work camps, roundups and so forth. In some cases they have attained considerable success, held national offices that carried some prestige, spoken to large audiences. Some have held churches in their undergraduate days. Some have even been successful as "boy" or "youth evangelists." It is quite an adjustment to move from a position of leadership and recognition to just a member of a class. It can be even more difficult when students who had no such recognition seem to do as well or better in class.

There are some who follow the traditional pattern of the theological student. He had always intended to go into the ministry. He was active in the church, took an undergraduate major in religion and came immediately to seminary. Usually all his friends were pretheological students and his activities were related to the church. Such a student may be shocked at some of the ideas and the behavior of those who come from quite a different background. Much that he finds in seminary may be a duplication of what he had in college. Somewhere in his experience he needs contact with those who have had no religious background. He needs to learn to understand the world of people who have little religious interest, for these will be the ones he will serve.

Some have had no religious training or background whatever. Their undergraduate majors may have been in business, science or the arts. Their decisions for the ministry came late in their academic careers or even after their undergraduate work was completed. Some made such decisions while in the service and determined to enter seminary when they were discharged. Rather than having to duplicate college work in seminary, they remain without sufficient background. A seminary professor of Biblical studies may assume a knowledge of Biblical content, but this student has no such knowledge. He may be taking prerequisites in philosophy at the same time he is taking theology. This is an added problem, but many students make the transition, and some make it very well.

Then there are the career men. It is not that they are uninterested in religion—they are, but to them religion is one way they can get ahead. (The minstry provides a certain amount of status [with some groups] in our culture.) They vie for offices. They have great ambitions. They want to be successful. They cultivate the right people. They aim at becoming the bishop, or they seek election to national offices. They strive for recognition and awards—and sometimes attain them.

And others have strong humanitarian drives, like the boy we mentioned earlier, who wanted to help people. They score high on the "P" score (pastoral concerns). Some of these students are attracted to religious social service. Some go into institutional chaplaincy. Some desire to be specialists in pastoral counseling. Some leave the ministry for professional training in psychology or case work. It is to be hoped that more men will relate this drive to the actual work of the parish ministry.

The reformers, the prophets have great social concerns. They often become impatient with the church. They are highly critical (and not without reason) of the inertia within local congregations and denominational boards. Again, it is to be hoped that such a drive will be channeled into the work of the church and not separated from it.

Some are in seminary because of some special interest, such as religious art, religious drama, religious television, religious journalism or research. The seminary is the only place for these persons to receive training, but often seminaries are not equipped, either in personnel or equipment, to provide the specialized training they desire. Resultingly, they often experience frustration as they pursue studies not in line with their major interests. There is a further complication at the point of placement. It is easy to place a man in a church, but the number of openings in religious drama, religious television or religious research is very few.

Some students in seminary are quite confused as to what they want to do. They are honestly seeking. On the completion of college, rather than go into something they were unsure of, they went to seminary. Some, on the other hand, have found that seminary and the ministry were not what they expected (again we see the need for adequate knowledge and information). Some are frankly disillusioned. Many are facing an intense struggle. Some are struggling with personal doubts, some with guilt—all of which creates a feeling of unworthiness. Again we emphasize that this need not be too serious, providing they get help and work their problems through.

There are those who might be classified as "rebels" within the church. They are in revolt against the church and society. Their motivation is sometimes good, sometimes symptomatic of personal conflicts that need to be resolved. Rebels have made some real contributions in the past. We don't want to lose them. They can cause some real feelings of frustration for faculty members at times.

Some obviously are misfits. They do not belong in seminary. Perhaps they do not have the ability to do the work. It is nothing against them. It is only to recognize that if a seminary is a graduate school, a certain amount of intellectual stability is required. To permit some of these students to continue only to fail is to be unfair to them and to the church. Possibly moral and emotional problems seem to make them unfit for the church. A difficult situation arises when, after a student has completed the required work for a degree, the faculty feels it cannot recommend him for a position. The "misfits" need help, and the earlier the better. Some can be saved for the church; but some may need to be rerouted.

An increasing number of older students are in our seminaries. It consists of men who have been in business or one of the professions and have decided to return to school to prepare for the ministry. Most have been very active as laymen; in fact, usually this is what has stimulated them to want to do such work full-time. Older than the rest of the student body, they may have problems related to their family's accepting the adjustment and lower standard of living. Although active in a Bible class, they probably have had no acquaintance with the critical study of the Scripture that is carried on in seminary. Sometimes this is shocking, sometimes challenging. They may have held positions of some responsibility. It is quite an adjustment to change from being a district manager to a class member in which fellow students are the age of one's children. Again it points up the need for counseling both before and after such a decision.

Each of these group descriptions has been presented because it illustrates a problem that may benefit from counseling. It does not mean to imply that all seminary students need counseling. Some do not. Since this is a book on counseling we are dealing with these things that require or lead to counseling. It does not imply that all who seek counseling are seriously maladjusted or weak. It may be a sign of strength. Problems of seminary students are probably not basically different from those of other graduate students. They, too, have academic, financial, vocational, family and emotional problems.

Seminary is a graduate school. It requires an A.B. or its equivalent for admission, yet many students have not learned how to study. They make a poor stewardship of time. Most of them are serving in a student church or in some other form of field work. Often there is a very real conflict for time. They find both competing for their time and energy. Many find it difficult to play both roles—a student through the week, a pastor on weekends.

At times this raises vocational problems. A student church can be a discouraging experience. At times it is a disillusioning experience. If the church is small (as most such churches are) there is limited leadership. The congregation may not challenge his efforts, and if its members are used to a long line of student ministers, they see him as a boy who will be there for a short time and then be gone. Some students tend to judge the ministry by this experience. They may get into difficulty with their church boards or leaders because they have not yet learned the art of interpersonal relationships. Some are subject to rather severe criticism. On occasion a student pastor will be released (fired is a more accurate term). All such experiences can cause personal problems that would benefit from counseling. Both the present situation and the student's usefulness in the future are involved.

Many theological students are quite confused vocationally. They are not sure of their call. They are not sure what they want to do or be. This is evident by the number who drop out of seminary and the rather large number who leave the ministry after a rather brief try at it.

A large percentage of theological students are married. As in any other segment of the population they have marital problems, too—only they seem to worry about it more. Imbued as they are with high ideals and lofty expectations, they feel very anxious and guilty at the presence of tension or difficulty. It seems to be an implication that their home isn't Christian, that they should be above such things. Frequently all they need is some reassurance that such tensions are normal, a part of being human, and can be worked out.

Theological students' wives have some unique problems. Many do not accept the role of the minister's wife. Some needlessly fear a stereotype or have a false image of a minister's wife. Some feel guilty because they do not measure up to all the ideal descriptions that are found in the books on "How to be a Successful Minister's Wife." As one fine young woman said, "I don't have a deep devotional life. I don't read the Bible every day. I can't lead meetings. I don't want to be a handicap to my husband—I guess I just don't fit."

Some of these wives had no intention of becoming ministers' wives. They fell in love with young men who were in prelaw, premedicine or studying as business majors. Later, often after marriage, the husband changed his vocational plans. His wife may or may not share his dedication to the church. She may or may not want to teach school for three years to put him through seminary. This is especially true of the wives of older men who have been in business for a few years. This means that the wife has to give up her home, income, standard of living and so forth. This is not easy for some.

Many wives seem jealous of the church. The church demands all of the husband's time. He expresses great devotion to the church. He loves the church. She feels slighted and left out. The church becomes almost a third party, but it is an unfair rival. It's wrong to be critical of the church, but she resents the time she spends alone. She wants his love and devotion, too.

All of these preceding paragraphs emphasize the fact that the theological student also has emotional problems—whether more or less than other graduate students we are not prepared to say. The Niebuhr report says, "The theological student tends to be self-critical and introspective to a greater extent than some other graduate students."[30] Yet Dr. Gothard Booth, a psychiatrist who has done extensive work in testing and counseling theological students, says, "There is some evidence that serious nervous breakdowns occur less frequently in the clergy than in the average population, only half as often as in lawyers or physicians."[31]

It is only to be expected that seminarians will have religious problems also. The theological student must study and analyze his faith and live by it at the same time, and that is not easy. Some, especially if from rather rigid and conservative backgrounds, are likely to be shocked by some of the critical findings in Biblical studies. Many students are troubled about their own devotional life. It does not seem adequate. It does not do for them what they think it ought to do. Some want the seminary to teach them how to pray.

Lest this be misunderstood, again we point out: Theological students are no worse than students in other graduate schools. The results in later life would indicate that many of them fare better. This is a book on counseling. Counseling deals with problems. There are problems in seminaries—some that require extensive counseling and therapy. The majority clear up quickly. The students come to insights quickly. They are well motivated. They understand the counseling process.

The majority are well adjusted and work through their difficulties to find a useful ministry.

Part II

UTILIZING THE RESOURCES OF THE CAMPUS

CHAPTER THREE

PERSONNEL And COUNSELING SERVICES

If the pastor is sincere in his concern for students, he will utilize all the resources the campus has to offer. He will never attempt to do himself what someone else can do better. He is one among many who are working with students. Faculty, deans of men and women, personnel workers, counselors, psychologists, psychometrists, speech therapists, reading specialists and many others—all these people have had advanced training in special fields. They also are concerned about the students. It is inevitable that they must work together, refer to one another, share valuable information with each other. This cooperation is not always as good as we wish it were, but there is no question that this is the trend. The pastor is either going to be a part of the team or going to be left out.

The good of the students makes it imperative that the pastor understand the services available and the philosophy and methodology of those responsible for the services. Seymour Smith was writing of the university chaplain but his words apply equally well to all religious workers. ". . . The chaplain needs insight into the philosophy, policy, and the practices of the dean's office or other personnel organization, an insight which probably best comes through close working relationships. Without this knowledge of the practicalities of the situation within which he must work, the chaplain may find himself doing more harm than good as he helps students find their way through to the solution of the problems they are facing."[1] Here is the pastor's great opportunity. The pastor on a campus has a definite advantage over the pastor in the average community. He has referral resources available such as no other religious worker has. It is up to him to understand them and utilize them.

Personnel services on a campus cover a multitude of activities. These would include such things as orientation procedures, housing and food services, student activities, fraternity and sorority supervision, student government, discipline, campus security, traffic regulation, counseling and guidance, testing, health services, financial aid, student employment and placement, advising veterans (sometimes) and foreign students and maintaining contacts with the community and with parents. The administrative pattern varies with different schools. Certain responsibilities are assigned to different departments and different heads.

It is only natural that different patterns of organization and procedure exist. Campuses have different needs, and the whole field is new. The first course in student personnel work was not offered until 1916. Specialists in personnel work speak much of "the personnel point of view." This does not refer to the services offered as much as to the philosophy behind them. It is a philosophy that recognizes individual differences and personal needs. It stresses the fact that a student's education may be influenced as much by what happens outside the class as what happens in. It emphasizes that each student must be seen as a unique individual and dealt with as a whole, in terms of his personal, emotional and social needs, as well as his intellectual needs. Campuses differ not only in the organization for personnel services but in the importance they attach to such matters.

The "personnel point of view" is growing in most areas, and all of these responsibilities have to be carried on by someone on every campus. The three that are most closely related to the pastor are the counseling service, the testing service and the administration of discipline.

The Counseling Service

Student counseling as a specialty is new. Student counseling as concern for the individual student, his problems and his growth, is as old as higher education. For generations there was little need for a special counseling service. For the first fifty years of its history the attendance at Harvard seldom exceeded twenty students and the president did much of the teaching. In the early days of education the friendly teacher, professor or dean who gave advice and took a personal interest in students was all that the college offered and possibly all that it needed.

In the last two or three decades, however, a combination of circumstances, both on the campus and off, have made the counseling service and the specialist in student counseling a necessity. On the campus the phenomenal increase in enrollment, the amazing expansion of the curriculum and coeducation have all combined to create an unprecedented situation. From 1890 to 1924, the general population increased by 78 percent; the college population increased 445 percent. From 1850 to 1950, the general population tripled; the college population increased ninety times. As late as 1900, only two schools claimed as many as 2,000 students; now many schools enroll more than 20,000. With the increase in student body came a corresponding increase in faculty. The old concept of the friendly teacher, the personal interest and personal contact were gone. Increasing the size of the student body also increased the anonymity, the pressure, the tensions—all of which lead to problems.

The curriculum expanded almost as rapidly as the enrollment. This made a student's choice of a major and of a career much more complicated and confusing. Contrast a student's choice in Phillips Brooks' day with that of a student at Harvard today.

Coeducation, which barely existed before the Civil War, became almost universally accepted, with the exception of a few schools that only admit students of one sex. With coeducation came new social and moral problems. In order to "protect" women students, new officers were added to the staff. Occasionally known as "wardens," they later came to be designated "deans of women."

At the same time that needs were increasing on the campus, a combination of new developments off the campus was to have a real influence on university personnel work and student counseling. We can't do more than list them here. The interesting thing is that they all appeared more or less simultaneously, often unrelated, but were to be combined in their influence on student counseling.

The vocational guidance movement under Frank Parsons created a new emphasis and offered some important techniques. The guidance movement in secondary education was somewhat parallel to, yet separate from, college personnel work but demonstrated some needs and possibilities. The mental hygiene movement made everyone aware of the importance of emotions and the necessity of considering the student as a whole. The testing movement made available standardized techniques and procedures by which a student could be evaluated and plans could be made. Research in educational and general psychology discovered much about the learning process and the possibility of providing help in such areas as study, reading and speech. Progress in psychiatry and depth psychology created an awareness of the significance of unconscious influences and the possibility of therapy and help for disturbed students. A renewed interest in counseling, the controversy between the clinical and client-centered approaches to counseling—all created a new interest in counseling procedures and did much to improve methods and techniques.

All of these influences, growing out of the need on the one hand and the improved insights and methods on the other, created a new area of specialization, a new vocation—the counselor of students. Many people follow this profession. Their training consists of a background of general psychology, usually progressing to the master's degree, and preferably the doctoral level, in special training in counseling and guidance.

Whereas the controversy mentioned above is no longer as acute as it once was, there still exist differences in philosophy among student counselors. Some make much more use of test information than others. Some tend to lean more to therapeutic orientation, while others see their function more in terms of guidance, with a strong emphasis on educational and vocational problems. The general trend is toward a more eclectic position; in fact, this is so true that it is difficult to tell from a college catalog just what actually is available. All college catalogs stress that counseling is provided for students.

Melvene Hardee reports a survey of the kinds of counseling eighty-nine institutions of higher learning provided for their students. Thirteen different kinds were listed. In order of frequency with which they were mentioned, they were: placement counseling, health counseling, vocational counseling, educational counseling, psychological services, counseling veterans, residence counseling, religious counseling, remedial reading, speech and hearing, marriage and family-adjustment counseling, psychiatric services, foreign student advisement.[2]

Many of these items we are including in other categories, but the list illustrates the wide range and also the diversity from campus to campus. While eighty of the eighty-nine schools listed placement counseling, only forty-nine included counseling on marriage and family adjustment. Seventy-eight schools provide vocational counseling, but only thirty-five offer psychiatric services.

Again, the answer is for the pastor to know his own campus and, more important, to know the counselors individually, their orientation, their points of view, their willingness to work cooperatively.

This leads to a final question. Are university counselors willing to cooperate with the clergy? The answer, in the main, is "Yes." They do hope the pastor will be well trained in counseling and will recognize his limitations. When he meets these qualifications, they welcome the opportunity to provide such cooperation.

We made a study of university counselors and personnel workers to determine their attitudes on the place of religious workers in the counseling and guidance of students. The following responses are typical:

A dean of students said, "I believe it to be vital and essential, especially in these times. Particularly useful as a supplement to other counseling."

A professor of psychology and director of counseling, "Many personal problems have a religious flavor. Many people feel 'easier' in consulting a religious worker than others."

A director of counseling, "Obviously it is or should be one of the major justifications of their existence."

A director of student personnel and guidance, "The religious counselor has a definite place in the total counseling program in that there are many problems that arise in which the religious counselor is able to establish rapport much easier than other counselors."

A counselor in a student counseling center, "He plays, in my opinion, a very important role, just as do others outside the general clinical counseling center."

A "Yes" was occasionally qualified with a statement similar to one of these:

"Provided they are appropriately trained and professionally oriented."

"Provided they recognize their own possible functions and limitations."

"I am assuming they will be trained in counseling, not merely full of pious urges to help others."

"Only if they are well trained in counseling. If so trained, there is more than enough work for all."

Such statements indicate that professional counselors feel that the religious counselor not only has a rightful place but a very important one. In only rare instances was there any expression of an unwillingness to cooperate. On the contrary, they welcomed the pastor, expressing a common desire that he be well trained. With this we would thoroughly agree.

It is worth noting that these same counselors said that few pastors sought their cooperation. A closer relationship between pastor and university counselors is a real need on the campus.

The Testing Service

The testing service is usually operated by the counseling service or, at least, is closely related to it. Occasionally it is a function of the psychology department, but this is incidental for our purposes. The important point is that on most campuses some form of psychological testing takes place. This is a valuable source of information for the pastor, giving information about a student's academic potential, his previous academic record, his interests, aptitudes and personality.

At the time of his entrance to the school the incoming freshman is given a battery of tests. The specific tests differ, depending upon the preference of the psychometrists at the school, but the general areas measured are about the same. These would include such things as English placement, reading skill and comprehension, mental ability, vocational interest and personality adjustment. These are usually group tests that can be simultaneously administered to a large number of students. In special cases, when the group tests are inconclusive or when academic or personal problems that need special attention or evaluation arise, then individual tests, such as the Wechsler-Bellevue Test of Mental Ability or the Rohrschach test for personality adjustment, may be administered.

Such tests, or any psychological tests, for that matter, should only be administered and interpreted by those who are trained and qualified to do so. This is another advantage for the pastor who is working on the campus. Such persons are available. Their services can be obtained with no cost to the pastor or to the student.

This has many values for the pastor. It helps him to understand the individual student by providing him with information he can secure in no other way. It is information that is objective, standardized and presented in meaningful forms. The pastor does not have to guess at a student's abilities or depend on mere observation. Through standardized tests he has information by means of which he can compare any individual student in relation to the students with whom he is competing on this campus, or against national norms.

It provides him with information quickly. A pastor could conceivably gain an understanding of a student's abilities, interests and personality over a period of time, but it would require weeks or even months to speak with any degree of accuracy. The testing bureau probably already has such information on file; if not, a battery of tests administered in one afternoon would reveal it quickly and accurately. This is especially useful when contacts are not frequent. The pastor does not see the student every day in class; he does not hear him recite but does need some means of evaluating his potential and his ability. Tests can provide such information.

Dr. E. G. Williamson says, "The trained counselor does not rely solely upon the impressions resulting from a short interview with a student."[3] Frequently the pastor does, but he shouldn't when other information is available.

Such information may prevent the pastor from making mistakes. It provides a check on his observation and his other methods. A student's trouble in school may be due to the fact that he does not have the ability; it may be due to a lack of interest; it may be because of poor reading; it may be that he is emotionally disturbed. The procedures a pastor would follow depend greatly upon which is the reason.

One student who was failing academically went to the pastor because he was considering dropping out of school. His grades indicated that this might be necessary. It was proposed that a test of mental ability might help in making the decision. The test revealed that he was in the top half of the top 1 percent of the population. His problem was not lack of ability; it was personal and emotional. Here again the pastor needs a check on his own observation. If he is counseling with an emotionally disturbed student, a good test can help him determine whether the disturbance is of such severity that he should be referred to the psychiatric services, or whether it is something with which he can deal.

Tests can be a real service in educational and vocational guidance, especially in making plans for the future. If a student expresses a desire to become a medical missionary, it is important to know if he can pass chemistry and if he is likely to be admitted to medical school. If a student raises the question about pursuing a Ph.D. degree, it is important to know whether or not his scholastic aptitude is such that this is a realistic goal. Not to secure such information when it is available borders on a violation of professional ethics.

For these and other reasons, the pastor needs to understand tests, their nature, their use, their values and their limitations. Throughout this volume we have stressed the need for the pastor to work cooperatively with other campus personnel, professors, counselors, personnel workers and so forth. They think in terms of these findings. If the pastor is to work with them, he must also.

He must realize certain principles that, too numerous to mention here, can be found in any good book on testing in education. He should know that individual tests are more accurate than group tests, that mental ability tests measure the potential a person has for scholastic success. They do not measure motivation or personality. They say what he can do, not what he will do. The pastor should remember that each test was constructed for a definite purpose and should be used only for that purpose. Vocational interest tests measure interest, not aptitude or ability; personality tests are subject to change as the student's experiences change. All testing should be thorough.

The pastor should realize that all tests have limitations and are subject to error. Whenever there is doubt, the student should be retested. This is especially true when some life decision or career plan is being discussed. All tests should be used with caution and always in connection with other means of evaluation, such as observation and interview.

Certain ethics should be strictly adhered to. If the pastor is going to secure such information, he should secure the student's permission to do so. This is usually granted. The student knows that the pastor wants the information to understand and help him, and he is usually quite willing for the pastor to know about his test results.

When the pastor is counseling a student and a need for further test information is indicated (that is, tests beyond those he received upon entering the university), it is well for the student to share in the test selection. This may be done with the pastor or the testing center or, in some cases, by all three.

Some people have raised the question, "Should the pastor be trained in testing and should he administer these tests himself?" As a rule the answer is "No." It isn't necessary, in the first place. This is certainly true on a college campus. It is very time-consuming, in the second place. It requires considerable equipment, expense and facilities, in the third place. The pastor isn't a psychometrist and doesn't need to be.

Furthermore, there is some evidence to the effect that his counseling will be more effective if he doesn't give tests. There is nothing wrong with a pastor's giving tests if he is trained to do so, but this may not be the best counseling procedure. Many people feel that counseling is more effective when someone other than the counselor does the testing. Testing, in many respects, is rather threatening and judgmental, whereas counseling is understanding and permissive. The two roles may conflict.

The interpretation of the test findings would depend upon the pastor's training, the policies of the testing service and the relationship of the two.

It is better when test information is worked into the counseling process. Test findings should only be given in the form and to the degree that the student can understand and accept them. Test results should be presented in such a way that the student has opportunity to express his feelings and concern about them. On occasion it may be desirable to give tests over a period of time, for this reason. When test information indicates a change of plans or program, this should be done cautiously and with much care. The ultimate purpose of all testing is to help the student understand himself and make the most satisfactory adjustment and most effective use of his life.

Again we face the questions: Do those in the testing field welcome the cooperation of the pastor? Will they provide the information? Will they accept referrals for special services? In the great majority of cases, the answer is "Yes." They do expect the pastor to use the information professionally and confidentially. They may not reveal exact scores, and we do not feel that they should. They will usually give an interpretation that helps the pastor to understand the nature of the problem or the situation with which he is dealing.

The unfortunate thing is that so few pastors seek such information. This is true not only of pastors, but of professors on the campus who work with students—often without checking on test information.

Our thesis is simply this: The pastor who accepts responsibility for the counseling and guidance of a student has the further responsibility of being thorough. He should make use of all information and every resource available. Tests are one source for understanding students—not the only one, but a very important one. There are some aspects of personality that no tests can measure. No important decisions, no evaluation of personality should be made on the basis of tests alone. Certainly no judgments should be based on the findings of one test alone. A combination of tests should be used, together with transcripts, observation, the interview and any other information that is available.

It is usually true that the more one understands about a person the more effectively he can help. After all, that is the pastor's purpose. Tests are one means by which he can help.

Discipline

Wherever you get a group of people together, you will have some behavior problems. Some form of discipline will be necessary. This is as true on a campus as it is any place else.

The kinds of discipline problems vary all the way from overparking and mild infractions of the rules, such as a failure to pay library fines on time, to actual violations of the law or serious cases of sex perversion. The file of any discipline committee's cases over a reasonable period of time will include such items as: traffic violations, cheating on exams, plagiarism on papers and theses, stealing exams from professors' offices, drinking, gambling in the dormitories, changing official records, rowdyism in the dormitories, destruction of school property, fighting, forging names on library cards, refusal to keep hours in the girls' dormitories, stealing, failure to pay bills in the bookstore, forging parents' names on blanks, homosexuality, cutting material from books and periodicals, sex misconduct, excessive absences from class and so on.

This seems to be an imposing and frightening list, but it should be pointed out that students of today are probably no better or no worse than students of any other day,[4] and they certainly are no worse than any other subgroup in our society.

Williamson and Foley, in their book *Counseling and Discipline,* classify college disciplinary problems under seven major headings: (1) Financial irregularities, which would include nonpayment of debts, writing bad checks and so forth. (2) Minor misconduct, which may be the most frequent of all, including such considerations as interpersonal relations with the dorm supervisors and so forth (these may not be serious but, as the authors point out, may be of great nuisance value). (3) Disorderly conduct of a wide variety of types, such as reckless driving, use of intoxicants and destruction of property. (4) Sex misconduct—all the way from petting in public to serious immoral acts. (5) Theft and burglary, which may be on campus or off. (6) Misuse of privileges, such as selling nontransferable athletic tickets and loaning library cards to friends. (7) A group listed as miscellaneous, which includes a wide variety of things, such as misbehavior off the campus, living in unapproved housing and so forth.[5]

Any classification can only be for purposes of discussion. Each case must be seen as an individual one and handled accordingly. Different schools have different administrative procedures for handling such problems. These procedures usually are implemented by the dean of students, or someone with a similar title, who works with the deans of men and women, the campus police, if such are employed, and usually a larger committee that helps establish policy and works with individual cases. On some campuses this is a faculty committee whose members are selected because of their experience and training with such problems. Some schools utilize a student committee, student court, the student council or a similar group to help enforce discipline and, at times, determine action to be taken in certain areas. In many schools, faculty members and students work together in handling disciplinary problems.

Schools differ not only in their procedures in handling disciplinary problems but also in the general attitudes toward discipline. Some are very strict and impersonal, demanding strict adherence to the rules; others are more indulgent and lax. Attitudes toward cheating, for example, range all the way from demanding expulsion from school to a winking of the eye that takes it for granted. Some are almost primitive in their approach, while others emphasize counseling and rehabilitation.

This is a very knotty problem, loaded with emotion, filled with complexities and uncertainties—as is known by anyone ever called upon to serve in such capacities as those we have just mentioned. It is too complicated to describe here. Our concern is with the pastor and his relationship to students. At times the administration may call him in to work with a student. This is especially true if it happens to be one with whom he already has a good working relationship. This is a place where he can be of real service to both student and the administration. He has some real advantages in that he is not identified with the disciplinary action. He is not a threat as to grades or expulsion. Many times he can help when no one else can.

Other disciplinary situations may cause students to seek out the pastor. They have been placed on disciplinary probation. They have been warned, reprimanded, perhaps suspended or expelled. They may come to the pastor because of a sense of guilt, embarrassment, hostility or a combination of all of these. At this point the pastor has a real counseling job. He needs to be the one who can relieve the hostility and guilt, at times interpret the university, on occasion help preserve or re-establish relationships with parents and always work for the ultimate well-being of the student. He needs to help the student grow by this experience and not be defeated by it.

All of this underlines the necessity for the pastor to know his own campus and its regulations and attitudes. The pastor needs to understand both the student's problem and the school's problem. He needs always to hold up the idea that discipline should be redemptive. At times he can be of real help in working with individual students.

Whoever handles the problem—dean, counselor, faculty member, committee, pastor—should remember that misbehavior is a symptom of a need. All behavior is caused, and the causes of misbehavior are often complicated and deep. Some students, with sex deviations or chronic bad conduct, for example, may need specialized treatment.

All of these students need to be understood. Sometimes misbehavior is a result of frustrations and tensions of long standing. The group as a whole needs to be protected, but punishment has little, if any, therapeutic value.

As Dr. McKinney points out, "Undesirable acts are continued because they are at least partially satisfying. They may sometimes, of course, be immediately satisfying but later punishing. . . . Misbehavior arises often because the individual is thus not satisfying his needs in more effective ways. . . . When the individual can satisfy his needs in an effective manner, he will often abandon the symptoms which are self-defeating."[6]

This is what Williamson and Foley would call rehabilitative counseling. Williamson defines it in this way, "In disciplinary situations the counseling process helps the individual to face and gain insight into the consequences of his delinquent behavior, aids him in understanding the motivations and behavioral patterns which underlie his social conflict, and assists him in acquiring that personal growth and integration which facilitates the development of a more socially satisfactory and personally satisfying personality structure. In this sense, the counseling process promotes and effects rehabilitation and is, in its own right, a rehabilitative process."[7]

The pastor might call it a redemptive process, but it should be the goal of each. It should be pointed out, however, that it is much more than enforcing rules or agreeing on punishment. It requires all the wisdom, time and patience one possesses.

CHAPTER FOUR

THE FACULTY And SPECIAL SERVICES

The Faculty

If the pastor would serve his students he must work in cooperation with the faculty. The faculty on a college campus is composed of a group of specialists. Each is an authority, trained and qualified in some special area. They have information and can answer questions no pastor can possibly be expected to answer. This can be a great resource for the pastor. Sometimes he may seek the information himself. At times he may need to interpret to the student the faculty members' willingness to meet students individually and discuss these problems outside the classroom.

The faculty can also be a resource in certain areas of educational and vocational guidance. Its members can give firsthand information as to the nature of certain fields, the requirements regarding training, opportunities for the future and so forth. But this can create a problem. Their interest and enthusiasm for a field may cause them to overpersuade a student.

The faculty members are not only specialists in their own field of teaching but also are the best informed persons on the campus about such matters as planning an academic program. They know educational goals and objectives. They are acquainted with such matters as the content of courses, the sequence of courses, prerequisites, requirements for a major and a minor, necessities for a degree plan and all such matters as are related to working through an educational plan and program. Educational advising is a great skill, requiring much knowledge and experience. On most campuses this is a recognized part of the duties of the faculty.

There is no need for the pastor to be familiar with such technicalities; in fact, he is so likely to make mistakes on such subjects as prerequisites that he should only venture into this area when it is absolutely necessary; then he should have all definite plans and decisions checked to be sure he doesn't miss some technicality and complicate the student's program even more.

Some people would say that the pastor should never attempt to perform such a service. In the main, we would agree. This is the faculty's job. It is also true that this is an area in which students voice their most frequent complaints. They say that faculty members are too busy, too impersonal, too interested in their own fields to take the time to work out a plan that takes into account all of the student's feelings, concerns, uncertainties and confusion. All too often this is true. When a student comes to the pastor with such a problem, he can't turn him away, but he should try to help him get the assistance he needs and double-check all decisions that are made.

The faculty can be a real resource for personal counseling, as well as for academic advising. It can be a real help in assisting the pastor in understanding the individual student. Faculty members see him in a different setting, often for a more extensive period of time. They can interpret his strengths and weaknesses, his possibilities and limitations, his general attitudes and response to situations. The faculty member is interested in the student, too, and when a pastor, chaplain or other religious worker seeks him out, he usually finds an ally.

Many faculty members do a lot of personal counseling, and some do it very effectively. For generations this was the only counseling done on any of our campuses. It is only fair to recognize that there is great variation among the attitudes of faculty members toward counseling. Some teachers have no interest in or aptitude for counseling at all. Many are so involved in research or so preoccupied with their own fields of interest that they don't have time for students as individuals, unless possibly for some major who is working closely with them.

As Dr. Williamson has pointed out, "Teachers who are predominantly subject-minded will have little except subject matter to discuss with students."[1] This does not mean that they do not make a contribution to the campus. They may be excellent professors. It means that they are not used as a resource for referral in counseling. They simply do not see this as part of their responsibility. To quote Williamson again, "There is little doubt that many college teachers see their responsibility toward the student strictly in terms of teaching. If students have problems not touched by their teaching, these are matters for which deans and chaplains and personnel specialists are hired. Why bother the professor?"[2]

Some professors even resent the academic advising mentioned in an earlier paragraph. They see it as an intrusion on their time. Since most schools expect this of all members of their faculties, some students have unpleasant and discouraging experiences.[3] These are the students who may seek out a pastor.

Faculty members have a wide variety of attitudes toward counseling as such. Many are quite unacquainted with its recent developments and almost totally ignorant of what can be accomplished. The lack of communication that can exist between specialists is sometimes astounding. Some see it as simply giving good advice and feel that anybody can counsel. Others misinterpret counseling as babying or pampering. They feel that each person should be a rugged individualist and not expect personal or vocational counseling. Many are quite unaware of the emotions and feelings of the students in their own classrooms and do not recognize the need for counseling. Some look on counseling as something of a fad and feel that personnel workers are, perhaps, necessary for a few students but not as a basic part of a program on the campus. Some welcome counseling services because it relieves them of all responsibilities. They don't need to spend time with students. Such professors do not have a good relationship with the university counseling service or with pastors on or near the campus.

All of which is to say that if the pastor is going to work with the faculty, he must know the faculty members as individuals. Some of them will welcome his referral of a student; others will not. Some will understand his purposes; others will not. As Hardee says in his book, the first step in dispelling suspicion and fostering cooperation between the personnel department and the faculty is for them to become acquainted with each other. The same is true of the pastor and the faculty. But he continues, "The greatest gain in the building of a working relationship among educators comes through the mutual deliberation of counselor and teacher on the problems of a particular student."[4]

When the pastor does take advantage of the opportunity of working with a faculty member about some student with whom both are mutually concerned, he will find that he not only helps that student but has also prepared the way for similar opportunities in the future and, on not a few occasions, may find that he is discussing the faculty member's problems as well.

Special Services

On most campuses there is a wide variety of special services which have been provided to meet particular needs. These are usually provided by specialists in their fields and are available to the student either at no cost or at a nominal fee. The pastor must know what these services are. Frequently a problem comes to his attention first. The student may come to him because he has a study problem, a health problem or a financial problem, as the case may be. No one should attempt what someone else can do better. It is unfortunate when a student receives this advice, "Get in there and study harder," when there are study habits clinics that really can help him scientifically and, perhaps, a reading course that will double his rate of reading.

It seems strange but students are often unaware of such services or are hesitant to accept them. The pastor's task is to know about them, to interpret them and frequently to refer to them. On occasion he will need to work cooperatively with them for the benefit of an individual.

These services vary with the campus. Some are under the direction of the personnel department; some are sponsored by the departments of education, psychology or fine arts. It varies from campus to campus. Here we can only refer briefly to some of the more common ones.

Speech Clinics

It is estimated that about 10 percent of all young people have speech problems.[5] The student with a speech defect has a very real personal and emotional difficulty. Communication is all-important in social relations and is almost a necessity in some fields of educational and vocational achievement. The emotional accompaniments of a speech defect may be more severe than the practical ones.

The stutterer or the student with an impediment in his speech suffers from anxiety. He fears disapproval and feels "different." Usually these problems have existed since childhood, causing a long history of frustration and embarrassment. As one student, who had been a stutterer since preschool days, said, "I have been hurt so many times. I ran home from school crying too many times to recite in class now and get hurt again."

The important thing is that speech is learned behavior and usually can be helped. Many schools have speech therapists who teach in the speech department and are available to students.

The pastor may be the one to persuade the student that such efforts are worthwhile and can produce results. At times he can be of real assistance to the therapist by providing the encouragement and motivation that keeps the student in the program. Speech therapy is a long, slow process. Sometimes a student must be content with little gain and slow progress. If he will persist, he can often make significant gains. This may be as important, in terms of personal adjustment, as extensive counseling. It may contribute as much to his success as his academic program.

Study Habits Clinics

The psychology of learning has been subjected to as much research by educational psychologists as any one subject. It has been proven by innumerable research studies that there are definite methods, techniques and habits of study that are more effective than others. We discussed this in the chapter on academic problems. Many students are not aware of these methods; in fact, very few students use them very extensively. One study of superior students revealed that very few utilized the best methods of preparing for an exam, scheduled their time efficiently or organized their material most effectively. It has been demonstrated that the average student can raise his grade average and increase his satisfaction in studying as such by discovering the methods that produce the best results.

Some schools sponsor study habits clinics. These are of value not only to the students on probation, but also to good students who could be accomplishing far more if they utilized the methods that would best use their time and talents.

Reading Clinics

The ability to read rapidly and well is probably the most basic single skill necessary for academic success and achievement. Orientation tests of freshmen students reveal a difference in reading rate from a hundred and some words a minute to more than five hundred words a minute. It is obvious that the student who only reads one to two hundred words a minute is at a disadvantage. It takes him twice as long to complete the same assignments. On the other hand, the student who reads rapidly has that much time to do extra reading, to participate in other campus activities, to work or to rest.

The encouraging thing is that one's reading rate can be improved, sometimes dramatically. It is not at all unusual for a student to double or triple his reading rate under proper guidance. It is also encouraging to note that increasing the reading rate does not decrease comprehension but usually increases it.

Many campuses have remedial reading or developmental reading courses in which a student can benefit from trained help in developing reading skills.

Health Services

All schools have some form of health service. Students become ill, and some provision has to be made for the diagnosis and treatment of disease. This usually is furnished to the student for a modest fee, which may be included in the general fees paid at the time of registration. When a pastor is counseling a student who complains of physical symptoms, he should always refer him to the health center— unless the student lives at home. Then, of course, the family physician can be consulted. Campuses differ as to the degree of medical care and infirmary facilities they provide.

Some schools include psychiatric services in the medical center.

Psychiatrists may serve on a part-time basis or, in the case of a large university, may be full-time. Any sudden or severe changes in behavior, signs of severe depression, extreme mood swings, lack of relations to reality should be referred for diagnosis and possible treatment.

Scholarships and Loans

Many students have financial problems; in fact, at times it would seem that this is the major problem. There are occasions when the financial problem may be the determining factor in whether or not a student stays in school. A large percentage of students earn a major portion of their educational expenses; some earn all of it. There are some who support a wife and family in the process.

The problems are frequently brought to the attention of the pastor first. Unless we are referring to the rather rare (we hope) case in which the pastor lends a student $10.00 to see him through a temporary emergency, it is better for the pastor to work with those in the university who are responsible for loans and scholarships. For this reason he needs to know who such people are and what services are available. Students or their parents may be unaware that scholarship and loan funds are available. This, too, differs greatly from campus to campus. Some schools make use of all scholarships available, while others have some which are unsought and unclaimed.

At their best, such services are seen not merely as a means of imparting funds but as "financial counseling." Dr. George Risty, Director of the Bureau of Student Loans and Scholarships at the University of Minnesota, describes it as "advertising a student concerning sources of financial aid and opportunities for self-help and guiding him in making his own intelligent decisions in planning and executing his financial program with due consideration of his capacities, interests, health, study habits, and attitudes. The financial counselor assists the student in determining his needs and in planning his budget, and thereby he obtains a realistic picture of his financial responsibilities and commitments in comparison with his earning capacity and his assets. Whatever aid is provided should be in such a form and under such terms that the student views the assistance in the light of a privilege rather than as a right or charity."[6]

Employment Services

Most schools provide some form of employment services. These would include odd jobs for board and room, campus jobs that can apply on fees and tuition, part-time work in the community, summer jobs and placement in full-time positions after graduation.

As we have pointed out, all these services vary from campus to campus. The pastor must know what services are available on his campus, what the requirements are, what fees are involved and what the limitations are. This is another advantage that the worker with students has in contrast with the pastor in the parish. In the parish, if such services are available at all, they are widely scattered, with little chance for communication—and subject often to excessive fees. The pastor has them all concentrated on one campus, where communication between workers is relatively simple, with no expense or only a modest fee.

Part III

THE PASTOR AND HIS METHODS

CHAPTER FIVE

COUNSELING METHODS And PROCEDURES

The counseling that a pastor does with students takes place at many levels and has a wide variety of expressions. Some is very informal—almost casual. It takes place over a coke, at a social gathering, after a committee meeting or when a student just drops by the office or the pastor's home. It may be rather formal, structured and scheduled—such as from 4:00 to 5:00 P.M. Tuesday at the office. Some sessions may be brief, complete in one conversation or one interview. Some may extend over an entire semester or, for that matter, over several semesters.

One may be just as important and far-reaching as another. To speak of different levels or different expressions does not mean that one type is more significant than the other. All are significant, for all affect the student's present well-being and his future.

Some of these contacts may rightfully be termed (1) *guidance*. Here the pastor helps the student evaluate choices, seek information, make decisions. These may be relatively minor choices, like the choice of a book to read or a course to take (although we recognize this may not be a minor choice). It may be a major life decision, like the choice of an entire course of study, the choice of a career or of a life partner. In other cases he is engaged not so much in guidance as in (2) *counseling*, although in actual experience the two overlap. Here he is not so much concerned about working out plans as he is working through feelings. As we have said earlier, all students experience feelings of inadequacy, doubt, guilt, unworthiness and so forth. Some of these are surface problems or situational difficulties that create a temporary disturbance or irritation. Some may be deep-rooted and crippling. They deal with a student's basic concept of himself, his ultimate loyalties. In some such situations it might be characterized as therapy, although we use the word with great caution. Medical men and psychotherapists do not want pastors practicing therapy in one sense—and rightfully so. On the other hand, providing relief from guilt, overcoming hostilities and restoring a divided self are healing to the student's torn self—very therapeutic. Here the pastor is helping the student work through feelings of inadequacy, hostility, guilt and fear. He is helping him to understand and accept himself.

At times the pastor may have a (3) *pastoral care* relationship with students. Students, too, face experiences of sickness, trouble and sorrow. On such occasions the pastor may simply "stand by," providing a supporting, sustaining ministry.

In any case, whether the relationship is formal or informal, short-term or long-term, whether the need is for guidance, counseling or support, two things are present: the felt need on the part of the student, and the desire to help on the part of the pastor.

The Counseling Relationship

The ability to provide this help depends upon many different things. Actually, with any one student it depends upon a combination of many things—attitudes, methods, techniques, procedures and philosophies. While all these things are significant, the relationship is the most important of all. If a pastor has a good relationship with a student, the student will be helped, even if the pastor makes mistakes in technique. If he has a poor relationship, even the best techniques will become mere mechanics.

The counseling relationship is characterized by two all-important words: *acceptance* and *understanding*.

If a pastor is going to help a student, he has to understand him. This means primarily understanding his feelings. How does he "feel" about his grades, his relationship with his girl, his relationship with his parents, his relationship with himself? How does he feel about his future plans? Perhaps a better statement would be that the pastor has to *try* to understand. No one ever fully understands another; but, if the student feels that the pastor is *trying* to understand, this in itself will help. Sometimes the feeling that someone is trying to understand is all that is needed.

In his effort to understand, the pastor utilizes test scores, observation in informal groups, conversation—any sources that are available. He is always trying to sense, or enter into, the inner frame of reference of the student.

The pastor guards against making snap judgments or premature attempts to diagnose either the student's needs or his problems. In all counseling it is axiomatic that the problem a person first presents may not be the one he is most concerned about at all. As Robinson points out, many students will use a "facade" problem to try out the counselor.[1] This may or may not be a conscious process. It does not mean that the problem presented is not real. A student may stop by a pastor's office to talk about his grades, his study habits or his vocational choice. All these are respectable and accepted topics. Before he leaves, he is talking about his conflicts with his parents, his feelings on inadequacy and failure or his sense of guilt. It may take a long time to discover what the real problems are.

No matter what topic the student presents for discussion, the pastor tries to understand. This is not easy. It is hard for an adult to understand how it feels to be eighteen or nineteen. It is hard for one who is satisfied and content in his profession to understand how it feels to be uncertain and insecure and not know which way to turn. It is hard for one who has completed his academic work, perhaps with honors, to understand how it feels to fail. It is hard for one who long ago worked through his intellectual problems to understand the confusion and perplexity of doubt. This is the pastor's first responsibility—to try to understand.

As important as it is to understand a student, it is equally important to accept him. This means to accept him as he is, with all of his immaturity, all of his weaknesses and all of his faults. This means to accept him at his worst as well as at his best, and to see him as a worthy individual. It means to accept him if his behavior is not only questionable, but even if it is objectionable. It does not mean to accept or condone the behavior. It does mean to accept the student as a person.

Acceptance is one of the most meaningful words in both the theological and psychological literature of recent years. Perhaps it has been overworked. It is unfortunate if we let it become commonplace, for no word is more descriptive of the counseling relationship. One of the dangers is that it sounds so good and it seems so obvious that we often oversimplify it.

Dr. McKinney issues a warning to beginning counselors that applies to experienced counselors as well: "To be truly accepting requires considerable practice, long training, and conscientious re-education. For this reason let the counselor-in-training be cautioned that this new attitude of nonaggression and noncriticism will not be so easy to establish as he may think when he reads about it."[2]

Counseling is not a mechanical process. It depends upon a very sincere, profound interpersonal relationship of mutual trust and purpose. There is no other relationship quite like it. It is a relationship in which two people concentrate on the deepest concerns, anxieties, doubts, fears, ambitions, concerns, goals and purposes of the student. It is based on understanding and acceptance. Nothing need be excluded—guilt, resentment, hostility, hopes, dreams—all are shared and explored in the hope of finding a more mature, wholesome, redemptive outlook on life.

Such an understanding and accepting relationship is the most powerful thing a pastor has to offer.

Counseling Techniques

The interview.   We have not meant to minimize or depreciate techniques. Poor techniques can ruin a good interview. Such a simple matter as learning how to listen can sometimes work wonders with a student. Some years ago Dr. Henry Wieman said, "Black despair will scarcely clutch and hold for long if one can talk it out with a friend who understands." This has been verified a thousand times over. There is a skill in listening. One needs to know when to listen and when to talk, when to ask questions and when to reflect, how to open an interview and how to close it. These things have been discussed in many volumes and need not be repeated here.

The place of the interview even makes a difference. No student is going to reveal his innermost thoughts, his most embarrassing experiences if there is any possibility that he will be overheard or interrupted. Many student workers are at a disadvantage here. They do not have offices that insure privacy; they do not have a receptionist who can prevent interruptions.

The same is true of the time of the interview. A good counseling interview must take place at a time when both the student and the pastor are free from distractions and are able to relax and concentrate completely on the problem. Problems like those we have discussed in earlier portions of this study cannot be dealt with in a hurry. More difficult and complex problems may take several interviews.

Some pastors schedule regular counseling hours. This is time that they keep free for just such purposes. Sometimes it is difficult for students to come at these hours because of classes, labs or outside work, but a time must be found that is convenient for both.

With students, counseling is likely to be informal and unstructured. This is as it should be. Smith, in his study of the college chaplaincy, found that counseling of students takes place in drugstores, restaurants, at social gatherings, in fraternity and dormitory lounges, in the chaplains' homes, or in the students' rooms, or walking across the campus.[3] Such contacts may lead to more formal and structured conferences, to be sure. Some of these sessions might be called precounseling rather than counseling, but all are important.

Thus far we have not said much about the schools of counseling or the differences in philosophy. Again we refer to the literature because of the limitations of space. Many of the differences are rapidly breaking down. It is our conviction that the worker with students must be familiar with all schools of thought and choose those methods which seem most natural for him and most helpful with each individual—they may differ with different students and may also differ with the same student at different times, depending on the need.

Group guidance. The interview is not the only method the pastor can use. He has a great opportunity in that he also is related to a group. Professional counselors recognize the value of a group and are attempting to develop groups of their own. This is called group guidance, group counseling or group therapy. The pastor is fortunate in that he has a natural group already formed. It has a further advantage in that it is not identified as a therapy group or a problem group.

The group itself provides many resources—a sense of fellowship, a sense of acceptance and belonging, the chance to participate in group activities. Experiences of recreation, service and worship all have value that may relieve and help a student with personal problems. Much could be said about each of these, but again space does not permit.

We are thinking here of the value of the group for group guidance or group counseling. This may be done as an activity of the whole group, if it is small—or it may be done by separating into small groups for special purposes.

Group guidance has some advantages over individual counseling. It is an economy of time, for one thing. Information in such areas as marriage and the family, vocation and religious faith can be given to a group of students as effectively as to one student—sometimes more effectively. The group itself provides support. Students gain strength when they realize that other students are facing the same problems. The group also provides insights. Many times the suggestions of other students are as helpful as the pastor's. After all, they do have a high level of intelligence. Some people who cannot express themselves to an individual can do so in a group. Others may benefit, even if too shy to enter into the discussion. We recall one student who met with a group regularly for several months without saying a word. Finally he gained the courage to speak and said later that the group had done more for him than anything in his experience.

Group guidance does not take the place of individual counseling. It often leads to individual counseling. In some cases it is a strong ally of individual counseling. To be able to relate a student to a meaningful group may be as valuable a contribution as anything that could be done for him.

Referral. There are occasions when helping a student depends upon relating him to someone else on the campus or in the community who can render some specific or specialized service. The second section of this study deals with the resources of the campus. Our only emphasis here is that a referral is a real skill. It is an art that must be developed. All studies of pastoral counselors reveal that the percentage that make regular referrals is relatively small. No pastor should attempt to do something that someone else on the campus can do better. It is a mark of professional maturity to recognize one's own limitations. Our concern is always for the student's ultimate welfare. In each case the pastor should ask himself the questions: Do I have the time, the training and the relationship to render the student the help he needs? Is someone more qualified? Are there special areas in which I need help?

Sometimes the pastor may refer for complete treatment, as to a physician. He may refer for special service, as to a speech therapist or for special information like that which might be received from a battery of tests—but the pastor continues as the counselor. Sometimes he refers the student to another worker on the campus, such as a university counselor, and then the two share the responsibility of guiding the student.

One may ask the quesion, "Where does the pastor get contacts with students for counseling?" Counseling cannot be forced. If it is, it is not counseling. One can call a student in, if he thinks he is in need of help, but such a procedure has obvious disadvantages. If the student can be made aware that the pastor is genuinely interested and only desires to help, a counseling relationship may be established. At times this may be necessary. It is far better if the student comes of his own volition. Counseling by its very nature implies two people who mutually accept the relationship and are jointly seeking a solution to a problem.

Some pastors use other methods to acquaint students with the fact that they are available. Scheduling regular office hours for this purpose is one; printing brochures which describe the service, along with other activities such as worship and discussion groups is another. Much counseling grows out of informal contacts that may result from speeches, sermons or participation in group discussions like those previously mentioned. If in such groups the pastor seems to understand, if his attitudes are such that students feel they would be met with acceptance and maturity, they will come.

The best single way to establish a counseling ministry with students is to do a good job with the students who do come. They will tell others. Student referrals are probably the best referrals.

Another effective procedure is to work with other personnel workers and faculty. Once they realize a pastor is concerned and competent, they, too, will begin to refer students to him. Actually, the problem is not finding students to counsel; it is finding time and developing the skill to do it well.

The Goals of Counseling

The primary goals of counseling are to free the student from inhibiting, crippling emotions like inadequacy, anxiety, guilt and fear, and to help him develop attitudes of confidence, love and faith. The pastor attempts, through counseling, to reduce anxiety and to help create insight and self-understanding.

We do not mean to imply that the pastor eliminates all tension and all anxiety. That is not only impossible; it might not even be desirable. Some anxiety leads to growth and achievement. Anxiety before an exam may be a good thing. Anxiety is only bad when it is never relieved, when it is so strong that it is crippling, when it destroys the student's happiness and keeps him from doing his best. The goal of counseling is to relieve the anxiety that harms and make use of the anxiety that helps.

The counselor tries to help the student gain insight and self-understanding. The student needs to understand his own needs, his own weaknesses and his own strengths. It is the student's insight that is desired, not merely the counselor's. This may come slowly. It is a matter of feeling as much as knowledge. The student may gain more self-insight while he is talking and the counselor is listening than when the positions are reversed.

Another goal of counseling is to help the student arrive at those decisions, make those plans and acquire those skills by means which he will grow to his maximum potential, attain the fullest satisfaction in life and make the greatest contribution of which he is capable. Counseling is not only clearing up repressions and resolving conflicts, as important as these are. It is also helping an individual to rise to new levels of living and to dedicate his life to worthy causes and meeting important needs.

CHAPTER SIX

The PASTOR HIMSELF

A study was made of the methods and effectiveness of a group of psychotherapists to determine, if possible, what made for success in psychotherapy. Those studied represented different schools of thought; they followed different methods; they used different techniques. The determining factor did not seem to be the techniques that were used, for success with all of them was reported. The most important factors seemed to be whether or not the counselor had confidence in his methods and whether or not the patient had confidence in the counselor.

This would indicate, in terms of our study, that the pastor himself is the most important factor in the counseling process. If he has confidence in himself and in his methods, and if he is the kind of person in whom the students have confidence, he will help.

How does one gain such confidence in one's methods? It can only come from two sources: preparation and experience. By means of thorough training he gains a knowledge of what to do and a confidence that he can do it. By means of experience he has seen people work through their experiences and gain maturity and insight, and so he has the assurance that others can, too.

It is not dissimilar to the experience of the professor in the classroom. He starts the semester with a group of uninformed students. They could not possibly pass the final exam now. The teacher has confidence that if they will stay with him for the eighteen weeks and apply themselves, they can grow and learn. Not all of them will—for some may not be motivated to try. Nevertheless, he knows that most of them can and will, because he has seen it happen before. He has faith in his teaching methods and the learning process, so he proceeds with confidence.

So the pastor has confidence in the student's capacity to grow and to gain self-understanding, and he, too, proceeds with confidence.

The second question is even more important? How does he become the kind of person in whom the student has confidence? This is not separate from the other. Students will have confidence in the person who has confidence in himself. This does not mean overconfidence and conceit. Far from it! Students are quick to spot a show. It means that one is well aware of his own weaknesses and limitations. It means he is very humble. This is basic. Students are too sharp to be deceived. They will only place their confidence in one who is sincere.

It is obvious that one who would work with students must genuinely like them. He must have a real feeling of warmth. There are many people on a campus—professors, administrators and others—who are formal, inaccessible and often aloof. (This is not true of all, but of many.) The pastor, if he hopes to counsel with students, must be friendly and accessible.

Students are quick to classify people on the campus—professors, administrators, counselors and pastors. Some are known to be superficial and shallow; others are considered cold and unapproachable; some, competent and friendly. Some are considered partial to students in a particular field of study; some may be known for violating confidences; others, for their integrity. Some are considered too busy; others always have time to see a student. The reputation one achieves among students to a large extent determines the number of students that come to him and, somewhat, the nature of the problems they bring.

The pastor who would work with students must constantly be growing. He himself must be a student. Students themselves are engaged in this process. The pastor is not expected to know all the answers to all their questions. He must be facing the issues, also. He must share the experience, if he is to be competent to meet their needs and understand their process.

This is more than the increasing of the amount of one's knowledge, as important as this is. One should also be growing in his understanding of himself. This self-knowledge is a very vital and all-inclusive thing. It includes all that is implied in such words as maturity, adjustment, insight, self-understanding, self-acceptance.

One axiom in all counseling is that the counselor's ability to help others is in part dependent upon his ability to understand himself. We cannot help others find stability unless we have some stability ourselves. This is always incomplete and partial. No one ever attains it perfectly. The great therapists, the great pastors had their tensions and their anxieties, too. Read the biographies and see—there are no exceptions. But they attained some insight into them; they were in a process of becoming, to use a phrase of Dr. Gordon Allport's.

The pastor does not have to have infinite wisdom and perfect adjustment. He should understand himself, be friendly, like students, believe in their possibilities, be willing to give them time, be willing to make a real effort, to be patient, to work with others, at times, never to give up, and to have faith. If he has these qualifications, he will help.

When one rereads the preceding paragraph, it seems like quite an order—but it includes nothing that a good pastor cannot do or be. It is a lifelong process, to be sure. He should prepare himself to the best of his ability, but this preparation goes on throughout life, also. Recognizing this, a pastor can make a real contribution.

CHAPTER SEVEN

The PASTOR'S TRAINING

The importance of training cannot be overemphasized. This is true in any field. It is obvious in medicine, law or education. We want those who serve in these professions to be well trained. The welfare of their patients, their clients, their students depends upon their skill and their effectiveness. There is no place that this is more true than in counseling with students. A student's entire future, his contribution to society may be influenced by one counseling experience.

What training is considered essential for the pastor who is counseling with students? First, he is a pastor, so he should be a trained pastor. Basically, he is a theologian. He should have the minimum training provided by a Bachelor of Divinity degree or its equivalent. More training, if possible, would be beneficial. Second, he is a counselor. Since he accepts the responsibility of counseling, he should be trained as a counselor. He should be sufficiently grounded in psychology to understand human dynamics. He should be familiar with counseling methods and techniques. And finally, he is working on a campus. He should have some understanding of higher education, the learning theory and so forth. He should be particularly familiar with the field of religion in higher education.

This is the ideal. Such training requires a long time, considerable expense and great dedication. There are not many campuses where one can receive training in all three fields.

Many men have already completed their training and are now on the job. To those who are looking toward a student ministry as a career, we strongly recommend acquisition of a broad background in all three areas. We would suggest that those already in the field, take advantage of every opportunity to strengthen areas in which their formal training has been incomplete.

Much can be done by reading. If a pastor sets aside time to read one book a month, that would be twelve a year, or sixty in five years. He could become pretty well informed over such a period of time. He would become even more informed if he keeps records of his counseling, studies them and goes over them with other specialists, when they are mutually concerned about some student. He should study their methods and learn from their experiences and insights.

He can also continue his education in summer courses or institutes or in work on the campus on which he is working. Here is another opportunity and advantage the university pastor has at his very doorstep. There usually are courses available in such areas as counseling and guidance, psychology, sociology and philosophy—all of which have a bearing on his work. If he is on a campus that includes a seminary, he can do advanced work in the religious field. One course or so a semester should improve, not impair, his regular work, and over a period of a few years, would make him vastly more effective.

CONCLUSION

Early in this book we made reference to the fact that a minister befriended Washington Gladden, another challenged and counseled John R. Mott, a teacher exerted a very real influence on Harry Emerson Fosdick. Behind every life that has made a contribution has been someone who offered guidance, encouragement, friendship, counsel, understanding and support.

The leaders of tomorrow are on the campuses today. They have many needs and many problems. Their potential for good is beyond imagination. Here is the pastor's responsibility and opportunity. Who could ask for a greater challenge?

NOTES

INTRODUCTION

1. *Cf.* Frederic A. Birmingham, *The Ivy League Today* (New York: Thomas Y. Crowell Company, 1961), p. 3.
2. Harry Emerson Fosdick, *Successful Christian Living* (New York: Harper & Row, Publishers, Inc., 1937), p. 256. Used by permission.
3. Fosdick, *On Being Fit to Live With* (New York: Harper & Row, Publishers, Inc., 1946), pp. 54, 56.
4. Fosdick, *Hope of the World* (New York: Harper & Row, Publishers, Inc., 1933), p. 229.
5. See *Successful Christian Living*, p. 219.
6. Fosdick, "Personal Counseling and Preaching," *Pastoral Psychology*, March, 1962, p. 12.
7. Fosdick, *A Great Time to be Alive* (New York: Harper & Row, Publishers, Inc., 1944), pp. 112–13. Used by permission.
8. A. V. G. Allen, *Life and Letters of Phillips Brooks* (New York: E. P. Dutton & Co., Inc., 1901), I, 798.
9. Clarence Shedd, *The Church Follows Its Students* (New Haven: Yale University Press, 1938), p. 14.
10. *Ibid.*, p. 31.
11. Seymour Smith, *The American College Chaplaincy* (New York: Association Press, 1954), p. vii.
12. Basil Mathews, *John R. Mott, World Citizen* (New York: Harper & Row, Publishers, Inc., 1934), p. 161. Used by permission.
13. *Ibid.*, p. 151.
14. Edmund G. Williamson, *How to Counsel Students* (New York: McGraw-Hill Book Company, Inc., 1939), p. 2.
15. Fosdick, *Recollections* (Boston: Houghton Mifflin Company, 1909), pp. 29, 30.
16. *Cf.* Fosdick, *On Being Fit to Live With*, p. 190.
17. Gladden, *op. cit.*, p. 324.
18. George Adam Smith, *Life of Henry Drummond* (London: Hodder & Stoughton, Ltd., 1898), p. 278.
19. *Cf.* Mathews, *op. cit.*, pp. 32–33.
20. Kate Herner Mueller, *Student Personnel Work in Higher Education* (Boston: Houghton Mifflin Company, 1961), p. 97. Used by permission.
21. *Ibid.*, p. 30.
22. Florence Goodenough, *Mental Testing* (New York: Holt, Rinehart & Winston, 1949), p. 319.

23. *Cf.* Mueller, *op. cit.,* p. 30.
24. Quoted in Mueller, *op. cit.,* p. 458.
25. David Boroff, *Campus, U.S.A.* (New York: Harper & Row, Publishers, Inc., 1961), p. xiii.
26. Mueller, *op. cit.,* p. 37.
27. Boroff, *op. cit.*
28. Quoted in Percival W. Hutson, *The Guidance Function in Education* (New York: Appleton-Century-Crofts, Inc., 1958), p. 571.

CHAPTER 1

1. Williamson, *op cit.*
2. Gilbert Wrenn, *Student Personnel Work in College* (New York: The Ronald Press, 1951), pp. 9–10.
3. Francis R. Robinson, *Principles and Procedures in Student Counseling* (New York: Harper & Row, Publishers, Inc., 1950), p. 35.
4. *Cf.* M. E. Bennett, *College and Life* (New York: McGraw-Hill Book Company, Inc., 1933), p. 14.
5. *Cf.* Robinson, *op. cit.,* p. 8.
6. *Cf.* Hutson, *op. cit.,* p. 570.
7. Ruth Strang, *Educational Guidance* (New York: The Macmillan Company, 1948), pp. 15, 16.
8. Mueller, *op. cit.,* p. 96; Strang, *op. cit.,* p. 13.
9. See Russell L. Dicks, *Premarital Guidance* (Englewood Cliffs, N.J.: Prentice-Hall, Inc., 1963).
10. See R. Lofton Hudson, *Marital Counseling* (Englewood Cliffs, N.J.: Prentice-Hall, Inc., 1963).
11. *Cf.* Mueller, *op. cit.,* p. 430.
12. Richard and Katherine Gordon, *The Blight on the Ivy* (Englewood Cliffs, N.J.: Prentice-Hall, Inc., 1963), pp. 9, 12.
13. *Ibid.,* p. 13.
14. Chad Walsh, "Flat Minds, Kind Hearts and Fine Arts," *The Christian Scholar,* XXXVI, No. 2 (1953), p. 100.
15. Fred McKinney, *Counseling for Personal Adjustment in Schools and Colleges* (Boston: Houghton Mifflin Company, 1958), p. 316ff. Used by permission.
16. Robinson, *op. cit.,* pp. 4, 5.
17. Gladden, *op. cit.,* pp. 34–39.
18. Thornton Merriam, *Religious Counseling of University Students* (Washington, D.C.: American Council on Education, 1943), p. 40.
19. Daniel Jenkins, *Believing in God* (Philadelphia: Westminster Press, 1958), p. 11.
20. Merrimon Cuninggim, *The College Seeks Religion* (New Haven: Yale University Press, 1947), p. 250.
21. Henry Pitney Van Dusen, *God in Education* (New York: Charles Scribner's Sons, 1951), pp. 44, 52.
22. Murray Ross, *The Religious Beliefs of Youth* (New York: Association Press, 1950).
23. Merriam, *op. cit.,* p. 4.

Chapter 2

1. *Cf.* Maurice Freehill, *Gifted Children* (New York: The Macmillan Company, 1961), p. 354.
2. Joseph French, ed., *Educating the Gifted* (New York: Holt, Rinehart & Winston, Inc., 1959), p. 4.
3. Robert F. DeHaan and Robert J. Havighurst, *Educating Gifted Children* (Chicago: University of Chicago Press, 1961), p. 15.
4. Quoted in French, *op. cit.*, p. 331.
5. Edith Stedman, *The Gifted Student and Student Personnel Programs in Colleges and Universities* (Pasadena, California: Western Personnel Institute, 1956), p. 14.
6. Barbara S. Burks, *et al.*, *The Promise of Youth* (Stanford, California: Stanford University Press, 1925), p. 481.
7. Freehill, *op. cit.*, p. 389.
8. Terman as quoted in French, *op. cit.*, p. 49, from *American Psychologist*, June, 1954, pp. 221–30.
9. Stedman, *op. cit.*, p. 14.
10. *Cf.* Robinson, *op. cit.*
11. French, *op. cit.*, p. 332.
12. For exact figures, see Mueller, *op. cit.*, p. 484.
13. *Cf.* Theodore Blegen and Russell Cooper, *Counseling Foreign Students* (Washington, D.C.: American Council on Education, 1950), p. 1.
14. *Cf.* Mueller, *op. cit.*, p. 485.
15. Blegen and Cooper, *op. cit.*, p. 19.
16. *Ibid.*, p. 4.
17. Forrest J. Moore, "Trends in Counseling the Foreign Student," in *Trends in Student Personnel Work*, ed. E. G. Williamson (Minneapolis, Minnesota: University of Minnesota Press, 1950), p. 186. Copyright 1949 by University of Minnesota. Used by permission.
18. See Mueller, *op. cit.*, pp. 493–94.
19. *Ibid.*, p. 496.
20. B. Berelson, *Graduate Education in the United States* (New York: McGraw-Hill Book Company, Inc., 1960), p. 129.
21. *Ibid.*, p. 93.
22. Quoted in Frederic Ness, *A Guide to Graduate Study* (Washington, D.C.: American Council on Education, 1957), p. 48.
23. Berelson, *op. cit.*, p. 57.
24. Ness, *op. cit.*, p. 47.
25. *Ibid.*, p. 45.
26. Berelson, *op. cit.*, p. 171.
27. H. Richard Niebuhr, *et al.*, eds., *The Advancement of Theological Education* (New York: Harper & Row, Publishers, Inc., 1957), p. 11.
28. We use the term *ministry* here and throughout this chapter in the broadest sense. We mean any expression of the ministry, such as preaching, religious education, missions, and so forth.
29. *Ibid.*, p. 146ff.
30. *Ibid*, p. 164.

31. Gothard Booth, in an address presented at a Conference on Psychological Research, sponsored by the Board of Theological Education of the Lutheran Church in America, and titled, "Practical Conclusions from Twenty-four Years of Testing and Psychotherapy with Seminarians and Clergymen."

CHAPTER 3

1. Smith, *op. cit.,* p. 103.
2. Melvene Hardee, *The Faculty in College Counseling* (New York: McGraw-Hill Book Company, Inc., 1950), p. 12.
3. E. G. Williamson, *Counseling Adolescents* (New York: McGraw-Hill Book Company, Inc., 1950), p. 127.
4. *Cf.* Mueller, *op. cit.,* p. 384.
5. *Cf.* E. G. Williamson and John D. Foley, *Counseling and Discipline* (New York: McGraw-Hill Book Company, Inc., 1949), p. 84ff.
6. McKinney, *op. cit.,* p. 518.
7. Williamson and Foley, *op. cit.,* pp. 205–6.

CHAPTER 4

1. Williamson, *Counseling Adolescents,* p. 58.
2. *Ibid.,* p. 53.
3. Hardee made a study of 218 colleges and universities. All 218 institutions expected faculty members to do academic counseling. In 171, they did informal personal-social counseling. *Cf.* Hardee, *op. cit.,* p. 43.
4. *Ibid.,* p. 29.
5. *Cf.* Charles Palmer, *Speech and Hearing Problems* (Springfield, Illinois: Charles C. Thomas, Publisher, 1951), p. 5.
6. George Risty in Williamson, *Trends in Student Personnel Work,* p. 223.

CHAPTER 5

1. Robinson, *op. cit.,* p. 6.
2. McKinney, *op. cit.,* p. 233.
3. Smith, *op. cit.,* p. 95.

BIBLIOGRAPHY

I. *Student Personnel Work:* Those working with students should be familiar with the over-all student personnel program and point of view. He should know something of its organization and administration, in order to cooperate with it.

The Administration of Student Personnel Programs. Washington, D.C.: The American Council on Education, 1952.

ARBUCKLE, D. S., *Student Personnel Services in Higher Education.* New York: McGraw-Hill Book Company, Inc., 1953.

BARRY, RUTH and BEVERLY WOLF, *Modern Issues in Guidance-Personnel Work.* New York: Columbia University Press, 1959.

BRUMBAUGH, A. J. and RALPH F. BERDIE, *Student Personnel Programs in Transition.* Washington, D.C.: The American Council on Education, 1952.

BRUNSON, MAY, *Guidance: An Integrating Process in Education.* New York: Columbia University Press, 1959.

Guidance in Educational Institutions. Washington, D.C.: National Society for Study of Education, 1958.

LLOYD-JONES, ESTHER, *Student Personnel Work as Deeper Teaching.* New York: Harper & Row, Publishers, Inc., 1954.

MUELLER, KATE, *Student Personnel Work in Higher Education,* ed. by Gilbert Wrenn. Boston: Houghton Mifflin Company, 1961.

Trends in Student Personnel Work. Minneapolis: University of Minnesota Press, 1948.

WILLIAMSON, E. G., *Student Personnel Services in Colleges and Universities.* New York: McGraw-Hill Book Company, Inc., 1961.

WOOLF, M. D. and J. A., *The Student Personnel Program*. New York: McGraw-Hill Book Company, Inc., 1953.

WRENN, C. G., *Student Personnel Work in Colleges*. New York: The Ronald Press Company, 1951.

II. *Counseling and Guidance with Students*: The following books have been written primarily with the university counselor in mind. The religious worker should be familiar with them for two reasons: (1) to understand the method and approach of the university counselor so that he will understand such considerations as referral and how he can work cooperatively with him; (2) to improve his own methods.

ARBUCKLE, D. S., *Guidance and Counseling in the Classroom*. Boston: Allyn and Bacon, Inc., 1957.

BRUNSON, MAY, *Guidance: An Integrating Process in Education*. New York: Columbia University Press, 1959.

Guidance for the Academically Talented Student. Washington, D.C.: Conference on Guidance for the Academically Talented Student, 1961.

HAHN, MILTON E. and MALCOLM S. McLEAN, *Counseling Psychology*. New York: McGraw-Hill Book Company, Inc., 1955.

HEWER, VIVIAN, ed., *New Perspectives in Counseling*. Minneapolis: University of Minnesota Press, 1955.

JONES, A. J., *Principles of Guidance*. New York: McGraw-Hill Book Company, Inc., 1934.

KELLEY, J. A., *Guidance and Curriculum*. Englewood Cliffs, N.J.: Prentice-Hall, Inc., 1955.

McKINNEY, FRED, *Counseling for Personal Adjustment in Schools and Colleges*. Boston: Houghton Mifflin Company, 1958.

ROBINSON, F. P., *Principles and Procedures in Student Counseling*. New York: Harper & Row, Publishers, Inc., 1950.

ROTHNEY, JOHN W. M. and BERT ROENS, *Counseling the Individual Student*. New York: Holt, Rinehart & Winston, Inc., 1953.

SECHREST, CAROLYN A., *New Dimensions in Counseling Students*. New York: Columbia University Press, 1958.

SHOSTRAM, EVERETT L. and LAWRENCE M. BRAMMER, *Dynamics of the Counseling Process.* Englewood Cliffs, N.J.: Prentice-Hall, Inc., 1960.

STRANG, RUTH, *Counseling Techniques in Colleges and Secondary Schools.* New York: Harper & Row, Publishers, Inc., 1949.

————, *Educational Guidance.* New York: Harper & Row, Publishers, Inc., 1949.

WARTERS, JANE, *Techniques of Counseling.* New York: McGraw-Hill Book Company, Inc., 1954.

WILLIAMSON, E. G., *Counseling Adolescents.* New York: McGraw-Hill, Book Company, Inc., 1950.

III. *Testing in a Counseling Program:* University counselors utilize the findings of educational and psychological tests. The religious worker should be familiar with the field *not* as an administrator of tests, but so that he will understand their limitations and their use.

ANASTASI, ANNE, *Psychological Testing.* New York: The Macmillan Company, 1961.

CRONBACH, LEE J., *Essentials of Psychological Testing.* New York: Harper & Row, Publishers, Inc., 1960.

FREEMAN, FRANK S., *Theory and Practice of Psychological Testing.* New York: Holt, Rinehart & Winston, Inc., 1950.

FROELICH, CLIFFORD P., *Guidance Testing.* Chicago: Science Research Associates, Inc., 1957.

————, *Studying Students.* Chicago: Science Research Associates, Inc., 1957.

GOLDMAN, LEO, *Using Tests in Counseling.* New York: Appleton-Century-Crofts, Inc., 1961.

GREENE, H. A., *Measurement of Human Behavior.* New York: The Odyssey Press, Inc., 1952.

GOODENOUGH, FLORENCE, *Mental Testing.* New York: Holt, Rinehart & Winston, Inc., 1950.

IV. *Group Guidance:* Since much of a religious worker's contact with students is in groups, he should be familiar with some of the principles of group guidance.

HOPPOCK, ROBERT, *Group Guidance*. New York: McGraw-Hill Book Company, Inc., 1949.

KNOWLES, JOSEPH, *Group Counseling*. Englewood Cliffs, N.J.: Prentice-Hall, Inc., 1964.

STRANG, RUTH, *Group Work in Education*. New York: Harper & Row, Publishers, Inc., 1958.

WARTERS, JANE, *Group Guidance*. New York: McGraw-Hill Book Company, Inc., 1960.

V. *Religion in Higher Education:* Since the religious worker who deals with students works in the context of higher education, he should have some acquaintance with the thinking in the field of religion in higher education.

BUTTRICK, GEORGE A., *Biblical Thought and the Secular University*. Baton Rouge: Louisiana State University Press, 1960.

——, *Faith and Education*. Nashville: Abingdon Press, 1952.

FERRÉ, NELS, *Christian Faith and Higher Education*. New York: Harper & Row, Publishers, Inc., 1954.

JACOB, PHILIP E., *Changing Values in College*. New York: Harper & Row, Publishers, Inc., 1957.

LEFEVRE, PERRY, *The Christian Teacher*. Nashville: Abingdon Press, 1958.

MERRIAM, THORNTON W. *et al. Religious Counseling of College Students*. Washington, D.C.: The American Council on Education, 1943.

MOBERLY, WALTER, *Crisis in the University*. London: SCM Press, 1949.

SHEDD, C. P., *The Church Follows its Students*. New Haven: Yale University Press, 1938.

VAN DUSEN, HENRY P., *God in Education*. New York: Charles Scribner's Sons, 1951.

WALSH, CHAD, *Campus Gods on Trial*. New York: The Macmillan Company, 1953.

WALTER, ERICH A., ed., *Religion and the State University*. Ann Arbor: University of Michigan Press, 1958.

WILDER, AMOS M., ed., *Liberal Learning and Religion*. New York: Harper & Row, Publishers, Inc., 1951.

INDEX

DATE DUE

DATE DUE			
FEB 13 '91			
NOV 17 1997			